ON BORROW'S TRAIL
Wild Wales Then and Now

ON BORROW'S TRAIL

Wild Wales Then and Now

Hugh Olliff

First Impression – 2003

ISBN 1 84323 077 1

© Hugh Olliff

Hugh Olliff has asserted his right under the Copyright, Designs and Patents Act, 1988, to be identified as Author of this Work.

This book is published with the support of the
Arts Council of Wales.

Printed in Wales by
Gomer Press, Llandysul, Ceredigion

To the memory
of my Father

ACKNOWLEDGEMENTS

I am indebted to many for their help in the writing of this book. In particular, I should like to thank the staff at Gwasg Gomer, especially Ceri Wyn Jones and Francesca Rhydderch; Jack Jackson for his work on the preliminary design and layouts; Jane Whittle, Jim Roberts and Gordon Sherratt who kindly supplied illustrations; the staff who were so helpful at the Welsh National Library, Wrexham Heritage Services, Chester History and Heritage and the National Museums and Galleries of Wales; Dr Ann Ridler, Chairman of the George Borrow Society for her interest and encouragement; David Wyn Davies for permission to reproduce from *A Pictorial History of Machynlleth* and David Selwyn, Conservator at the Founders Library, Lampeter, for his informative correspondence. Also Penguin Books for permission to reproduce an extract from *The History of the Kings of Britain* by Geoffrey of Monmouth, translated by Lewis Thorpe (Penguin Classic, 1966); translation copyright © Lewis Thorpe, 1966. Finally, but most of all, I should like to thank my wife, Patricia Rhodes, without whose selfless and untiring support I could neither have begun nor completed this project. None of the above is responsible for any errors or deficiencies in the work which follows.

CONTENTS

INTRODUCTION

George Borrow was born on 5 July 1803, the second son of Thomas Borrow, a captain in the West Norfolk militia, and his wife Ann *née* Parfrement, an actress. The first years of his life were highly itinerant. His father's profession, a shortage of funds which prevented the maintenance of two households and the warlike times into which he was born all meant that the family was constantly on the move, usually from one army barracks to another. However, in 1816 after the conclusion of the Napoleonic Wars, they settled in Norwich and George was able to attend the Grammar School. He did not shine as a scholar, nor did he settle into his selected profession of the law. He was an unusual youth and a worry to his parents, but a youth with remarkable tendencies. He mingled with gypsies on Mousehold Heath, he discovered Welsh poetry.

Above all, he was interested in languages and his ability to acquire them was prodigious. While still in his teens, he came under the influence of the radical intellectual William Taylor who wrote of him '. . . He has the gift of tongues, and, though not yet eighteen, understands twelve languages'. Whatever qualifications we make about Borrow's linguistic achievements – and there are qualifications to be made, he did not, for instance, arrive in Wales the fluent Welsh speaker that he has sometimes been made out to be – he had a natural talent for learning languages.

In 1824, after the death of his father, George moved to London. Here his literary career can be said to have begun in earnest, although he was at first badly exploited and two decades were to pass before he achieved any real success. In 1833 he began work as an agent for the British and Foreign Bible Society, at first in Russia and later in Portugal and Spain where he was charged with the distribution of the New Testament in the Spanish language. His experiences in Spain furnished the material for his greatest commercial success, *The Bible in Spain*. So great were his sales that his popularity has been compared to that of Dickens and Thackeray.

During the 1830s and 1840s Borrow travelled widely, visiting Russia, Austro-Hungary, France, the Peninsula and many of the Mediterranean countries. Although he had spent some time in Ireland and Scotland during his boyhood, his Celtic journeys only really began in the 1850s. During this decade he travelled to Cornwall, twice to Wales, to the Isle of Man, to Scotland and to Ireland. His first Welsh publication, a translation of Ellis Wynne's *Visions of The Sleeping Bard* appeared in 1860 at his own expense, his publisher John Murray having declined to finance it. *Wild Wales* came out in 1862 and was only moderately successful to begin with. Even so, it has been through several editions since then and during the last decade two new editions have been produced by publishers in Wales.

What then accounts for the enduring popularity of *Wild Wales*, especially as Borrow in general is nowadays not very widely read? There is nothing particularly fashionable about him. His character has occasionally been attacked. He is rebuked for his egotism. A recent writer has described him as a 'one-man inquisition'. He can offend our political as well as our personal susceptibilities. As Cecil Price delicately puts it '. . . The list of his prejudices is rather long.'

This is certainly true. Take for example his attitude to religion. Passing an ancient building near Llangollen, Borrow is informed by his companion that it was Pengwern Hall, a former convent which had fallen into decay and was now used only as a barn. The contrast between the building's former and latter uses provokes in Borrow a terrific anti-Catholic outburst: 'Formerly it was a place devoted to gorgeous idolatry and obscene lust; now it is a quiet old barn in which hay and straw are placed, and broken tumbrels towed away: surely the hand of God is visible here?' His companion, a Calvinistic Methodist respectfully agrees with him. The modern reader is more likely to be shocked by this sort of religious venom.

We must place his prejudices in their context. The Act for Catholic Relief, which allowed Catholics to occupy most of the offices of state, was not passed until 1829 and then only as a result of pressures from Ireland. Dissenters of all creeds were not admitted to the Universities of Oxford and Cambridge until the 1850s. In mid-nineteenth century Britain anti-Catholicism was normal, not an aberration. Alas, we are not free of bitter sectarian division in our own times.

There is also more than a hint of illiberalism in his attitude to slavery. Quite early on in the book, in chapter 3, Borrow comes upon a black man on the city walls of Chester, a former slave from Antigua who now makes his living by speaking against slavery at religious meetings. Borrow's treatment of this man would be quite unacceptable today, but again we must place it in context, both personal and historical. Borrow had been piqued by the runaway success of the anti-slavery novel *Uncle Tom's Cabin*, published in 1851, the same year as his own *Lavengro* which had been a commercial failure. We must bear in mind that the Thirteenth Amendment, which declared slavery illegal in the United States, was not ratified until December 1865. At the time Borrow was writing, his views were still tenable.

In other ways he is much more appealing. His distaste for 'gentility nonsense', the hardening of social snobbery during the Victorian era, is quite acceptable now. He was kind to animals long before it became the norm to claim to be so. Who can forget his generosity to the church cat, or the young Lavengro's abhorrence of cruel blood sports?

The truth is though, that he was old fashioned, even in his own times. He has none of the radical or reforming zeal of some of his contemporaries. In some ways he was more a man of the eighteenth than the nineteenth century. His contempt for railways, his interest in prize-fighting, his horror of industrialism, his distaste for Victorian manners, his historical and literary tastes all hark back to the past.

It is also true that we like him despite his prejudices. In Wales he is said to be popular for his sympathetic treatment of the Welsh, their language and their culture. For myself, I like him because he is quite simply the liveliest of writers on Wales. He has brought together so much that is interesting about the country. He has produced a book which is, on the face of it a travelogue, and yet at the same time has the qualities of a novel. It is multi-layered and capable of almost inexhaustible analysis.

Wild Wales is a substantial book – 542 pages in the recent paperback edition – and this volume does not pretend to do it justice. For those who know Borrow, it is offered in the spirit of an illustrated companion. For those who have not yet read *Wild Wales,* it is offered as an invitation, both to the book and to the country.

CHAPTER ONE

Chester, Wrexham and Llangollen

On 27 July 1854, accompanied by his wife Mary and step-daughter Henrietta, Borrow set out by train for Wales. Two days later they arrived in Chester and put up in an old-fashioned inn, the Blue Bell in Northgate Street. For his family it was the prelude to a holiday in the picturesquely situated town of Llangollen; for Borrow it was the beginning of a pilgrimage to the shrines of the bards whom he revered and a journey into the romantic past of Wales. He also wanted, as he put it, 'to turn his knowledge of Welsh to some account.'

The Chester row is a broad arched stone gallery running parallel with the street within the facades of the houses; it is partly open on the side of the street, and just one storey above it...All the best shops in Chester are to be found in the rows.

Borrow describes Chester as

> An ancient town with walls and gates, a prison called a castle, built on the site of an ancient keep, an unpretending-looking red sandstone cathedral, two or three handsome churches, several good streets, and certain curious places called rows.

He tells us that the rows were originally built to defend the more prosperous merchants against the dangers of Welsh incursion, for all the best shops were to be found there:

> Should the mountaineers break into the town, as they frequently did, they might rifle some of the common shops, where their booty would be slight, but those which contained the most costly articles would be beyond their reach; for at the first alarm the doors of the passages, up which the stairs led, would be closed, and all access to the upper streets cut off.

Modern opinion is less inclined to stress defence in accounting for the origin of the Rows. Geology may have played a part. The unusually shallow bedrock at Chester prohibited the sinking of cellars, so these were built with their floors

Upon the walls it is possible to make the whole compass of the city, there being a good but narrow walk upon them.

almost at street level and the shops and houses above them were correspondingly raised, but only on the street side. At the backs of their houses people could walk out at ground level onto the accumulated rubble of Roman remains. Notably, the area covered by the Rows more or less coincides with the Roman fortress of *Deva*. The first mention of the Rows in the City's records occurs in 1330. However, it is thought that they began to develop towards the end of the 13th century when Edward I was campaigning against the Welsh. Presumably, therefore, the needs of defence cannot have been far from the minds of their builders.

Borrow made two circuits on the city walls, noting from the western one 'a noble view of the Welsh hills'. He stared long and hard in the direction of Mold, recalling to mind bloody stories of exile and revenge involving the warrior bard Lewis Glyn Cothi, the mayor of Chester and a ferocious chieftain called Rheinallt ap Gruffydd ap Bleddyn. It was on the walls too that he met the black Antiguan who had once been a slave, to whom we have referred in the introduction.

On a bustling Saturday night Borrow heard Welsh being spoken all around him in the streets. Chester still attracts many visitors from Wales, somewhat to the detriment of the economies of neighbouring Welsh towns, for its affluent and fashionable shopping district draws off much of the money which otherwise might be spent nearer to home. On Sunday the family attended a service in the cathedral. The 'unpretending' cathedral which Borrow describes was restored and much aggrandised by Sir George Gilbert Scott some twenty-four years later.

It was typical of Borrow's enthusiasm and energy that he spent part of the afternoon at an outdoor Methodist meeting. At the meeting we encounter something of his forthright manner of dealing with his fellows, for he roundly ticks off a man in the crowd for jeering at a temperance speaker. Not that Borrow was ever an apologist for teetotalism! This forthright manner is very characteristic: he is outspoken, robust and zestful in everything. Consider, for example, his disappointment with Chester's cheese:

To my horror the cheese had much the appearance of soap of the commonest kind, which indeed I found it much resembled in taste, on putting a small portion into my mouth. 'Ah,' said I, after I had opened the window and ejected the half-masticated morsel into the street; 'those who wish to regale on good Cheshire cheese must not come to Chester.'

And the ale too, detestable Chester ale, '...not lap for a dog, far less drink for a man', he similarly spits into the street. He would not have made a very good companion for the faint-hearted or those too delicately brought up.

In Chester too, Borrow visited an encampment of itinerants whose tents reminded him of those of gypsies. Gypsies were of course his stock in trade. Two of the books he had published to date, *The Zincali* and *Lavengro*, dealt with the subject and he was to spend part of his time in Wales working on *The Romany Rye*, the sequel to *Lavengro*. However, instead of gypsies he encountered a group of wandering Irish tinkers who mistook him for a priest or minister. This is a theme that will recur in *Wild Wales*. It has been suggested that Borrow deliberately introduced it to help give cohesion to an otherwise long and rambling narrative.

On Monday Mary and Henrietta went on by train to Llangollen, but Borrow followed on foot the next day. He crossed the River Allan and passed through Pulford and Marford, following the road which is now the B 5445. Ascending a hill he saw 'to the east the high lands of Cheshire, to the west the bold hills of Wales.' Here he met with a waggoner, a well-built man of prize-fighting

Chester's Cathedral today.

physique, to Borrow 'a genuine Saxon who, under Hengist subdued the plains of Lloegr and Britain.' He is referring to the story of Vortigern and Hengist which occurs in Geoffrey of Monmouth's *History of the Kings of Britain*. The Saxon leader Hengist lured the British king Vortigern, his generals and nobles with him, to an assembly on the pretence of talking peace terms. When the conference was gathered, and at a signal from Hengist, the Saxons fell on the unarmed Britons murdering them in great numbers. Vortigern himself was spared but only on condition that he forfeit his cities and his fortresses in exchange for his life. The Saxons then captured London:

> Next they took York, Lincoln and Winchester, ravaging the neighbouring countryside and attacking the peasantry, just as wolves attack sheep which the shepherds have forsaken. When Vortigern saw this horrible devastation, he fled to certain parts of Wales, not knowing what he could do against this accursed people.

Appropriately, at this point Borrow introduces the prophetic verses of Taliesin from which he has acquired his title 'Wild Wales':

> A serpent which coils,
> And with fury boils,
> From Germany coming with arm'd wings spread,
> Shall subdue and shall enthrall
> The broad Britain all,
> From the Lochlin ocean to Severn's bed.
>
> And British men
> Shall be captives then
> To strangers from Saxonia's strand;
> They shall praise their God, and hold
> Their language as of old,
> But except wild Wales they shall lose their land.

Brad y Cyllyll Hirion or Night of the Long Knives. The treachery of Hengist depicted in a wood engraving by Hugh Hughes in 1822. The picture was produced for an edition of *Drych y Prif Oesoedd*, a popular history of Wales first published in 1817. The figure on the left is Eldol who resisted valiantly with a stake, killing seventy Saxons and making good his escape.

Although this is Borrow's translation, these lines had also appeared in English with the publication of Lady Charlotte Guest's translation of *The Mabinogion* from 1838-49. Historically Taliesin was a praise poet of the late sixth century who flourished in the ancient lands of Wales, the Old North of Britain, but who may have been a native of Powys. *Hanes Taliesin*, or the *Story of Taliesin* was written much later. It may have developed during the ninth and tenth centuries, although Lady Charlotte worked from eighteenth-century sources, .

Borrow was now in Wales. He had once before stood on the border of the country but, though invited to do so, had declined to enter it. He would not do so until he had received due recognition for his translations of the poetry of Dafydd ap Gwilym:

> When I go into Wales, I should wish to go in a new suit of superfine black...mounted on a powerful steed, black and glossy . . . I should wish to see the Welshmen assembled on the border ready to welcome me with pipe and fiddle . . . and attend me to Wrexham, or even as far as Machynllaith . . . I should wish to be invited to a dinner at which all the bards should be present, and to be seated at the right hand of the president, who . . . should arise and . . . exclaim – 'Brethren and Welshmen, allow me to propose the health of my most respectable friend the translator of the odes of the great Ab Gwilym, the pride and glory of Wales.'
>
> (Lavengro pp 431-432)

Wishful indeed! And here he was. Alone and on foot. And he had not received, and was never to receive, the wished-for acclaim for his translations. But such romantic fantasies aside, there is a great sense of expectation about the opening chapters of *Wild Wales*, a sense of enthusiasm and anticipation as Borrow feels himself to be drawing ever closer to the country.

Arriving in Wrexham, Borrow made a hearty breakfast at the principal inn, The Wynnstay Arms, before wandering about the town. Though not very Welsh in appearance, it seemed to him a 'stirring bustling place, of much traffic, and of several thousand inhabitants.' Its lack of Welshness was confirmed for him by the church clerk who informed him that the weekly Welsh service was very poorly attended, and by a group of amiable idlers outside the church who assured him that the only Welsh words they knew were '*cwrw da*' or good beer. For Borrow, Wrexham's most remarkable object was its church whose most remarkable feature was its tower.

> Its tower is quadrangular, and is at least one hundred feet high; it has on its summit four little turrets, one at each corner, between each of which there are three spirelets, the middle most of the three the highest.

Leaving Wrexham and heading south for Llangollen, Borrow passed through Rhiwabon where he remarked on the ancient church. He was in industrial country now passing huge black colliery buildings, coal-laden carts and grimy men working amidst smoke and flame. He at last felt that he was properly in Wales for, on inquiring the name of a particular feature, he received the reply *'Dim Saesneg'* (No English). 'This is as it should be' he said to himself; 'I now feel I am in Wales.'

The tower of Wrexham Church is considered one of the wonders of Wales. This engraving, drawn by Gastineau in the 1820s, shows the grave (lower left) of Elihu Yale, founder of the American university which bears his name.

A stirring bustling place . . . of several thousand inhabitants.

CHAPTER TWO

Llangollen

Llangollen was to be the headquarters of the Borrow family until the middle of October. Borrow describes it thus:

> A small town or large village of white houses with slate roofs, it contains about two thousand inhabitants, and is situated principally on the southern side of the Dee. At its western end it has an ancient bridge and a modest unpretending church nearly at its centre. From some of the houses on the southern side there is a noble view. Dinas Bran and its mighty hill forming the principal objects. The view from the northern part of the town, which indeed is little more than a suburb, is not quite so grand, but is nevertheless highly interesting.

Borrow's wife had already found lodgings in a large cottage north of the river.

Llangollen in 1854 was much smaller than the town we know today. There had then been no development west of the line of Castle Street which itself was not built until the 1860s. The railway had not yet reached the town. Llangollen Station was not opened to passenger traffic until 1862, so Borrow's wife and daughter-in-law would have had to descend at Llangollen Road Station at Whitehurst. The town's most notable feature, the bridge over the River Dee, has seen many changes. The first stone bridge was built in 1345 by John Trevor I, Bishop of Saint Asaph. It was rebuilt in 1656

Llangollen's parish church, named after the seventh-century Saint Collen.

and a stone parapet was added at that time, quite possibly made of stone culled from Valle Crucis Abbey which was already in ruins. This was essentially the bridge which Borrow would have seen and walked upon. It was only eight feet wide in his day. It was widened in 1873 and again in 1969, and an archway was added on the northern side with the coming of the railway. Enlargements have however been sympathetic to the bridge's style, and the eastern side is original to the seventeenth century

The church too was smaller than the present building. The south aisle was built in 1863. At the same time the east end was enlarged and the west door was put in place in the tower. But if the church was modest, there was nothing 'unpretending', as Borrow might have put it, about the vicarage. An earlier vicar of the parish, the Reverend Robert Wynne-Eyton had been something of a 'squarson', a clergyman as much interested in maintaining the lifestyle of a country gentleman as in the spiritual welfare of his flock, and he had amply attended to his temporal comforts by building a splendid mansion on the northern bank of the river immediately neighbouring the Borrow's Dee Cottage. The incumbent in Borrow's time was named Edwards and his son William, whom Borrow describes as 'a fine intelligent young man', was the father of A.G. Edwards later to become the first Archbishop of Wales. The vicarage was sold off when the railway came to Llangollen and later became the Woodlands Hotel.

Two nineteenth-century views of Llangollen from watercolours in the private collection of L.G. Sherratt esq. Above, mid-century, looking southwest from a similar viewpoint to the photograph opposite. Below, W.G. Herdman's painting of the 1830s shows the Royal Hotel and river by moonlight.

Gone, gone are thy gates, Dinas Bran on the height! So declaimed Borrow, translating from the lines of a seventeenth-century bard. Romantically depicted by Turner, less romantically described by Jan Morris as 'Like a set of rotting old teeth', the castle has stood in ruins for many hundreds of years.

Borrow began his explorations with a series of short walks in the immediate vicinity of Llangollen. First he ascended to the ruins of Castell Dinas Brân on the northern hill of Llangollen. The castle was built by Madog ap Gruffydd some time before 1236, though there have been fortifications on this site ever since the Bronze Age. It had already been ruined for many hundreds of years by the time Borrow made his ascent, but there is apparently no hard evidence to support the popular belief that it was sacked by Owain Glyndŵr. For much of the nineteenth century there was a shelter on the summit of Dinas Brân where refreshments were available for visitors, but this was probably not operating in 1854. Today, in early morning before the crowds arrive, it is possible to find the ruins quite deserted, except perhaps for the occasional scurrying mountaineering rabbit. The view from the top is glorious, but even in clear weather it is easy to appreciate Borrow's inability to make out the summit of Snowdon.

Beneath Dinas Brân, Llangollen has grown out of all proportion to anything Borrow could have imagined. Gone are the crowds of begging children who followed Borrow all the way to the top of Dinas Brân. Gone too are the mowers he met on the hillside. Their successors have left these neat rows and uniformly packaged silage bags, a composition in the morning light.

Borrow next turned his attention to the canal, exploring along the towpath to the west. He refers to it as the 'Camlas', which is Welsh for canal, but properly speaking it is the Llangollen Branch of the Shropshire Union Canal. He is lavish in his praise for this waterway. In his boyhood he had seen the great aqueduct which carries the canal at Stockport and it had 'filled his mind with wonder'. Now he acclaims the canal as 'the grand work of England, [which] yields to nothing in the world of the kind, with the exception of the grand canal of China.' The locals too were impressed by the canal's constructions, though they may have preferred to claim them for Wales. Later he was to walk

eastwards along the towpath in the company of his local guide, John Jones. Reaching the Pont Cysyllte after a four-mile walk, John Jones calls the great aqueduct built by Thomas Telford in 1795-1805 'the finest bridge in the world, and no wonder, if what the common people say be true, namely that every stone cost a golden sovereign.'

Borrow records conversations with bargemen, one of whom informed him that slates were carried by canal all the way to Paddington. Slate was certainly one of the key exports. So too were lime, flour and ale. The commercial life of

Horseshoe Falls. *Few things are so beautiful in their origin as this canal*

the canal was however relatively short. Even in the nineteenth century industrial traffic was giving way to tourism and it remains possible to walk westwards along the towpath to the Horseshoe Falls, or to take a pleasure barge eastwards and ride the dizzying heights of Telford's aqueduct.

On the Monday evening of 7 August, Borrow walked with his wife and stepdaughter to view the ruins of Valle Crucis Abbey. He was not so much interested in the ruins themselves as in the fact that Iolo Goch, a bard closely associated with Owain Glyndŵr, was buried within the abbey precincts. Borrow describes how they found the abbey 'in a green meadow, in a corner near the north-west end of the valley of Llangollen.' He goes on to say 'The vale or glen, in which the abbey stands, takes its name from a certain ancient pillar or cross, called the pillar of Eliseg, and which is believed to have been raised over the body of an ancient British chieftain of that name, who perished in battle against the Saxons, about the middle of the tenth century'. On reaching the abbey, parts of which were then being used as a farmhouse, they were welcomed by a 'respectable dame' called Evans who unfortunately knew nothing of Iolo Goch, though she was able to show them a portrait of the much later poet Twm o'r Nant. Nor was a second lady, who guided them round the interior of the abbey, able to shed any light on the whereabouts of Iolo Goch's tomb. Borrow was very struck by this second lady, whose name Gordon Sherratt informs us in his *Illustrated History of Llangollen*, was Jane Lloyd. She was custodian of the ruins until 1881. To Borrow there was 'something singular about her' – 'She seemed to have a history of her own.' Her cottage, which was built as a summer house in the eighteenth century, still stands behind the ruins by the old monastic fish pond and it is still possible, as she directed, to cross the brook, climb the hill by the footpath and, turning right, follow the footpath which returns to Llangollen.

Pont Cysyllte

Pleasure craft at Llangollen

Whilst at the abbey, Borrow was pressed to taste the water from a holy well 'which in the time of the

The venerable abbey, slumbering in its green meadow.

popes was said to perform wonderful cures'. He courteously consented to try the water but could not resist a Protestant swipe at its supposed curative properties: 'We drank some of the *dwr santaidd* which tasted like any other water.'

Valle Crucis Abbey was by no means a thriving religious centre at the time of its dissolution in 1537. Shortly before then the king's commissioners had reported that only six monks were resident there. After the Dissolution the buildings themselves fell into decay as lead was stripped from the roof and stone was pillaged for other purposes. The abbey changed hands several times over subsequent years with some owners attempting to institute repairs, but the general picture was one of decay. Later in the eighteenth century the chapter house became a farmhouse and many of the buildings were used for farming purposes. By this time ownership had passed to the Coed Helen estate which retained it until the middle of the twentieth century. When Borrow visited, the estate had begun to take an interest in the preservation and restoration of the abbey. Today the ruins suffer the indignity of being surrounded by a camping and caravan site, but the buildings themselves are in the safe hands of Cadw. Their literature suggests that Borrow's quest to find the grave of Iolo Goch was a hopeless one: Owain Glyndŵr's great-grandfather is represented amongst the memorial sculpture, but there is no mention of his bard.

Borrow describes two further solitary excursions from Llangollen. The first up Geraint or Barber's Hill, so called because a long time ago a barber had been hanged there for the murder of his wife. Borrow had expected a glorious view of the vale, but was somewhat disappointed. He made his second and longer journey over the hill south from Llangollen to Pontfadog. Having been hospitably received by the people of *Ty'n-y-pistyll* or the house in the waterfall, he pursued his course through Gwernant Wood and via Carreg y Big, Llety Ifan and Plas-ym-minffordd to Pontfadog. There, seated with his ale in a small pub, he conversed with the woman of the house. Perhaps because he learned how quiet and isolated the hamlet was, he introduced the subject of the *Tylwyth Teg*, supernatural beings akin to fairies, though not necessarily benign. The woman had never encountered the *Tylwyth Teg*, but she had seen a corpse candle, a ghostly light which appears in the night to predict an imminent death. Pressed further she tells a story about 'knockers' and supernatural voices which foretold the death of her aunt. It is difficult to determine exactly what Borrow's attitude is to these tales of the supernatural. That is, to what extent he gives them credit. We will encounter many more of them in *Wild Wales*. My own opinion is that we should see him essentially as a collector. He delights in the story itself. He delights in the telling of it. The truth of it is of secondary importance. This attitude is expressed in another context. In conversation with a shoemaker about Madog, the Welshman fabled to have discovered America, the shoemaker asserts that Madog's tomb has been discovered in America and that his descendants are still to be found there speaking purer Welsh than the people of Wales. Borrow ventures to doubt this, but he says 'the idea is a pretty one; therefore cherish it.'

George Pickering's engraving of Valle Crucis predates Borrow's visit, but shows some of the features he describes. In the foreground is the fishpond beside which stands the cottage in which Jane Lloyd lived. To the left of the abbey church, smoke can be seen rising from the chapter house, then in use as a farmhouse.

The ninth-century Pillar of Eliseg stands on a mound a few hundred yards from the abbey and has shared some of the chequered fortunes of its neighbour. Originally surmounted by a cross and rising to a height of possibly twenty feet, it was thrown down and broken during the Civil War. Towards the end of the seventeenth century the already weathered and faded inscription was recorded by the antiquarian Edward Lhuyd. It tells us that the pillar was set up by Cyngen, last of the kings of Powys, in honour of his great grandfather Eliseg: 'It was Eliseg', the inscription continues, 'who united the inheritance of Powys (laid waste for nine years) out of the hand of the English with fire and sword.' In 1779 the shaft that we see today was replaced in its original socket and the Latin inscription which is still visible dates from that time.

Having at first been content to explore the countryside around Llangollen by solitary rambling, Borrow now decided to hire a guide. Partly for the sake of local knowledge, but also so that he could improve his grasp of colloquial Welsh. For this reason he requested his landlady to find him a guide who could speak no English, and such a one was provided in the person of John Jones. There are many attractive characters in *Wild Wales*, but few can be quite as likeable as John Jones. Borrow summarises him thus: 'I found my guide a first-rate walker and a good botanist . . . He was very honest, disinterested and exceedingly good-humoured.' There was occasional friction between the two men on religious matters, but overall Borrow 'found nothing to blame and much to admire in John Jones, the Calvinistic Methodist weaver of Llangollen.'

Borrow describes two major expeditions as well as other shorter journeys made with John Jones. The first of the longer journeys was made to Rhuthun, about fourteen miles from Llangollen in Borrow's estimation. The two men set out early on a bright morning and soon passing the Abbey and the column of Eliseg they toiled on up the road which is now the A452. Their stamina was remarkable for they crossed the whole of the Maesyrychen Mountain by way of the Horseshoe Pass and continued until they met the Wrexham to Rhuthun coach road, which is now the A525, before they stopped for breakfast. This they did at the Turf Tavern or *Tafarn Tywarchen*. The bread and cheese and ale were good, but quite a scene erupts when the woman of the house affects not to understand Borrow's Welsh.

The name of the tavern suggests its humble origins as a turf hovel. It was accepted custom before the encroachment of enclosure that people could build houses on common land. If a building was raised overnight and a fire lit in its hearth by morning, its builders won the right to occupancy. A little further on John Jones leads Borrow to a house built '*yn y hen dull* in the old fashion, of earth, flags, and wattles and in one night', explaining

> It was the custom of old when a house was to be built for the people to assemble, and to build it in one night of common materials, close at hand. The custom is not quite dead. I was at the building of this myself, and a merry building it was.

Borrow describes Rhuthun as a dull town, but one which possessed plenty of interest for him. This was on account of its connection with Owain Glyndŵr who sacked and burnt the town in 1400. Glyndŵr was not however able to take the castle which belonged to his enemy Reginald de Grey. That distinction belongs to Cromwell. Borrow visited the old part of the castle and recounts some of its surviving medieval features such as a drowning pit and a whipping post. The visitor today can quite easily avoid these horrors, but he must at least order lunch if not a room with en-suite bathroom if he wishes to visit, for the castle is now a smart hotel.

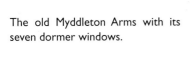
The old Myddleton Arms with its seven dormer windows.

We can assume that architecture was not Borrow's particular forte, for the buildings of Rhuthun are anything but dull. The old court house survives in the square, a late medieval building of half-timbered design, now occupied by the National Westminster Bank. In Castle Street the massively pillared Nantclwyd House dates from even earlier times. It is said to be one of only two buildings which survived the incendiary attentions of Glyndŵr. Of Dutch design and delightfully eccentric is the old Myddelton Arms, now part of the Castle Hotel, with its steeply pitched roof almost randomly scattered with seven dormer windows, known locally as the 'seven eyes of Rhuthun'. It was not here but at the Crossed Foxes that Borrow treated John Jones and himself to roast duck. The name has gone but the pub survives in Well Street as the 'Wynnstay Arms'. Its original name refers to the crossed foxes which form part of the family arms of the Williams-Wynns of Wynnstay. Borrow declared his duck to be capital and John Jones announced that he had never tasted better before. Indeed he had never eaten duck before. The five shillings a week of a weaver did not run to such luxuries.

The Wynnstay Arms at Rhuthun, where Borrow and John Jones enjoyed roast duck.

On the way back to Llangollen the pair stopped at the little Baptist chapel that Borrow had noted earlier in the day. This can be found about a mile south of Llanfair Dyffryn Clwyd, near to the village of Graig Fechan, but there is no trace of the memorial inscription which Borrow transcribes. At the head of the old road they paused at a tollgate and fell into conversation with its keepers. This prompts Borrow to ask John Jones whether he had ever heard of Rebecca. One suspects that Jones's reply is a later insertion by Borrow because the Rebecca riots took place almost exclusively in south-west Wales.

The second major expedition with John Jones was made to Pont y Meibion to discover the birthplace of the poet Huw Morys. Borrow and his companion crossed the hill to the south of Llangollen by way of *Allt y Badi*, Paddy Wood or Paddy Hill, so called because itinerant Irish had favoured it as a campsite. The two men had been this way before when Borrow had accompanied his guide on an errand to deliver weaving work. In fact on an even earlier occasion John Jones had been frightened out of his wits when on returning home at night he had passed a very fierce-looking band of Irish people. There were a great many people from Ireland in Wales in the 1850s. Many of them had been displaced from their homeland by the devastation of the famine of 1846. Very often it was the poorest who came to Wales for they were the ones who lacked the fare to cross the Atlantic to America.

Reaching Glyn Ceiriog, Borrow and his guide stopped for ale and then headed south into the valley of the Ceiriog. Borrow's description of the route is accurate and relatively easy to follow:

> The valley is very narrow, huge hills overhanging it on both sides, those on the east side lumpy and bare, those on the west precipitous, and partially clad with wood; the torrent Ceiriog runs down it, clinging to the east side; the road is tolerably good, and is to the west of the stream.

They passed the old fulling mill, now the Woolpack Arms, where the Ceiriog is confluent with the Teirw and in twenty minutes had reached a house on the right hand side, Erw Gerrig farm. They were welcomed by the people of the house, a stout dame and a girl of seventeen, and taken to see the chair of Huw Morys. This however was not easy to find for they first had to battle their way through a wilderness of shrubs, bramble and nettle. It was raining too. The modern literary pilgrim may be relieved to know that the chair has been moved to a more accessible spot, but it remains on private ground.

Having found the chair, after due ceremony, Borrow sat down in it and recited verses of Huw Morys. His little audience stood in the rain, amidst the nettles, and listened patiently and approvingly, winning from Borrow the commendation '. . . Enthusiasm is never scoffed at by the noble, simple-minded, genuine Welsh, whatever treatment it may receive from the coarse-hearted, sensual, selfish Saxon.' This is very typical of Borrow in *Wild Wales*. He is always at pains to point out how receptive the Welsh are, even or perhaps especially those Welsh of humble origin, to the poetry and literature of their country. In chapter 19 he reports how he had conversed with a miller's employee on the verses of Taliesin and discussed Huw Morys's birthplace with him. This had prompted him to comment 'What a difference . . . between a Welshman and an Englishman . . . What would a Suffolk miller's swain have said if I had repeated to him verses out of Beowulf or even Chaucer, and asked him about the

Huw Morys's chair today.

It now seems unlikely that Huw Morys (1622-1709) was born at Pont y Meibion but he moved here in about 1647 when he was twenty-five and spent much of his life working on the family farm. He was a devout Churchman and also a Royalist. However, so great was Republican Borrow's admiration for his 'ranting, roaring verses against the Roundheads' – rendered even more powerful no doubt by Morys's experience of seeing Cromwell's men sack the church at Llansilin – that he set aside his political disapproval.

residence of Skelton?' (The fifteenth to sixteenth-century poet John Skelton had written satires on Cardinal Wolsey and it is probably for this reason that Borrow selects him as an English counterpart of Huw Morys whose work had satirised Oliver Cromwell and his regime.)

A further example of this Welsh enthusiasm for their literature occurs when Borrow and John Jones were on their way back to Llangollen from Huw Morys's house. Stopping in at the pub by the fulling mill, they encountered a stonemason in an advanced state of intoxication. He was bemoaning the possibility that he might be called up for service in the militia. At first this man is all incoherence, but when he learns that Borrow has been to see the chair of Huw Morys and that he is a great admirer of *Eos Ceiriog*, the Ceiriog Nightingale, he springs up, thumping the table with his fist and declares 'I am somewhat drunk, but though I am a poor stone-mason, a private in the militia, and not so sober as I should be, I can repeat more of the songs of the *Eos* than any man alive, however great a gentleman . . .' He then proceeds to repeat the deathbed verses of the poet, 'hiccuping them up', as Borrow puts it while John Jones, 'much better acquainted with Welsh pronunciation', jots them down in Borrow's notebook. Borrow's comment again contrasts the Welsh and the English:

A scene in a public-house, yes! but in a Welsh public-house. Only think of a Suffolk toper repeating the death-bed verses of a poet; surely there is a considerable difference between the Celt and the Saxon.

Borrow's judgement is probably accurate and it remains the case today that the Welsh have more respect for their own literature than the English do for theirs. But he was also a great romantic and there was a sense in which he fantasised about the Welsh in a way that made them fit his image of them. It has been said of him by Professor John Davies that he was not particularly interested in contemporary Wales. He wanted to believe its people were immured in the world of Dafydd ap Gwilym, Huw Morys and Vicar Prichard, Twm o'r Nant and Goronwy Owen. By far the best-known verses of the time were the hymns of William Williams Pantycelyn, but an evangelical Methodist did not fit into Borrow's idea of a Welsh bard and he therefore ignored him.

CHAPTER THREE

Expedition to Anglesey and Snowdonia

On Sunday 27 August, Borrow set out on the first of his long expeditions which was to take him initially to Bangor, then to Anglesey, then back to Llangollen via Caernarfon, Beddgelert and Bala. His wife and stepdaughter accompanied him as far as Bangor, but they went by train while Borrow travelled on foot so that he should have 'perfect liberty of action, and enjoy the best opportunities of seeing the country.' He set out on a Sunday because he was 'anxious to observe the general demeanour of the people, in the interior of the country, on the Sabbath.' He followed the route of what is now the A5, but was then the important stagecoach route built by Telford to link Shrewsbury and Holyhead.

At Pont y Pandy he had his first opportunity to observe the religious demeanour of the people: it was disapproving of a man who walked about on the Sabbath and attended neither church nor chapel. However, he defended himself ably enough with reference to the gospels and learned of the existence of Owain Glyndŵr's mount which lay a little way further along his route.

> The mount of Owen Glendower stands close upon the southern bank of the Dee, and is nearly covered with trees of various kinds. It is about thirty feet high from the plain and about the same diameter at the top. A deep black pool of the river which here runs far beneath the surface of the field, purls and twists under the northern side, which is very steep, though several large oaks spring out of it.

Borrow's description still serves well today, though the line of the Llangollen Steam Railway now runs along the northern bank of the river, and the view of the mount from the road has not been improved by the presence of advertisements beneath it. In conversation with a local farmer, a conversation held in Welsh, Borrow says that he believes the mount to be man-made, but that it was raised long before Glyndŵr's time, probably as the burial mound over some long dead king. Even so, Glyndŵr may have used it as a lookout point to watch for his enemies. There are earthworks in the ground beneath the mound and modern opinion has it that these are Glyndŵr's fortifications. The mound itself predates him.

At about two o'clock Borrow reached Corwen and retired to an inn aptly named the 'Owen Glendower' for his habitual refreshment. The inn still retains its name and the fact that this is Glyndŵr territory is amplified by a statue of the man himself which stands across the road.

The statue was commissioned by the local council and first erected in 1995, but had to be withdrawn from public view amidst a storm of criticism and threats of vandalism. It is certainly a very unheroic representation of the great Welsh patriot. However, it was reinstated on a higher plinth in 1996 and today the squat bronze figure stares unseeingly across the square, subject to the occasional petty insult of a traffic cone hat, but by and large tolerated and even regarded with affection by the locals. If the statue lacks dignity it is not the only occasion on which Glyndŵr has been treated with less than absolute reverence. In *King Henry IV Part One*, Shakespeare's Henry Hotspur teases the future prince:

Owain Glyndŵr's Mount stands on private ground, but can be viewed from the adjacent main road. Above, his bronze statue in nearby Corwen

Glendower . . . and at my birth
              The frame and huge foundation of the earth
              Shaked like a coward.

Hotspur   Why, so it would have done
              At the same season, if your mother's cat
              Had but kittened, though yourself had never been born.

Glendower I say the earth did shake when I was born.

Hotspur   And I say the earth was not of my mind,
              If you suppose as fearing you it shook.

Glendower The heavens were all on fire, the earth did tremble.

Hotspur   O! then the earth shook to see the heavens on fire,
              And not in fear of your nativity.

(Act III Scene I)

Borrow travelled on, crossing first the Dee and then the River Alwen. The corn harvest was being gathered in. After some miles he came to a beautiful wild country scattered with cottages and he stopped to admire the scenery from a looking-place. At a house called *Pen y Bont* he spoke to an elderly blind woman called Catherine Hughes who named what Borrow describes as a 'kind of devil's bridge' as *Pont y Glyn bin* or the bridge of the glen of trouble. This is typical of the sort of minor inaccuracy of which the reader of *Wild Wales* must be wary for *blin*, not *bin*, is the Welsh for troublesome. In fact, not even this knowledge will equip the traveller to find the bridge for on the Ordnance Survey map it is marked as Pont y Glyn *diffwys* which the *Modern Welsh Dictionary* has as 'wild, steep or wonderful'. Following Catherine Hughes's directions, Borrow was able to fulfil his desire to observe the population at their devotions, for he dropped into a chapel a little further up the road. He was courteously received and allowed to listen to the congregation's prayers and hymns. He has perhaps justly been accused of being vain about his linguistic powers, but he was capable of modesty too. In this instance, for example, he describes his Welsh as far inferior to the chapel usher's.

Borrow stopped that night at the White Lion in Cerrig y Drudion, which is a small quiet village now removed somewhat from the main road. Here he met Dr Jones, a country doctor who in former years had served in the West Indies, but who had returned to spend his latter years in what he plainly regarded as the obscurity of his birthplace. The Doctor was delighted with Borrow's company, pleased both by his knowledge of Welsh literature and by his ability to speak the language. One can imagine how quiet a spot this must have seemed in the middle of the nineteenth century to a man both travelled and

Pont Glyn Diffwys. *Below me was the deep narrow glen or ravine down which a mountain torrent roared and foamed.* The bridge and ravine are bypassed by the main road today, but they can be found at OS 992444.

The White Lion at Cerrig y Drudion.

educated. Together the two conversed on Welsh poetry and other subjects until the doctor was called away on professional business. The landlady too was tickled to be entertaining a Welsh-speaking Englishman and she introduced him to an Italian weather-glass or barometer salesman who had also mastered some of the language.

Borrow's claim to have mastered the difficulties of Welsh poetry by twice going through (William) Owen Pughe's translation of *Paradise Lost* with the original by his side is a startling one, but partly borne out by the survival of Borrow's copy of Pughe's work in the National Library of Wales. However, he would also have had access to Welsh grammars, one by Pughe himself and a second, more reliable, by Sion Rhydderch.

The following morning Borrow set out to walk the thirty-four miles to Bangor. The first man he met was an Irish Catholic, raggedly dressed, gammy legged and carrying a fiddle. Borrow certainly makes this character dance to his own tune. He asks the Irishman to play him 'Croppies Lie Down', a Protestant song, but the fiddler refuses to play to such 'blackguard Orange words', offering instead 'Croppies Get Up'. However, the offer of a shilling soon elicits the requested tune, the implication being that the Catholic's loyalties are easily bought. It is very likely that much of this incident is fabrication and that it has much more to do with Borrow's opinions on the Irish Question than with any real life encounter. The late Sir Angus Fraser has observed that in Borrow's diary '. . . There is a reference on the day in question to a man on crutches (none too compatible with fiddle-playing) and then a gap, so there is no clue to how much of the episode may have been invented. One suspects, most if not all of it.' Fraser follows Edward Thomas who in *George Borrow: The Man and his Books* commends the scene as 'an admirable piece of imagination'.

Pentrefoelas.

Walking on over 'flat uninteresting country' Borrow eventually came to Pentrefoelas, the principal seat of Sir Watkin Williams Wynn. A woman seated by the roadside knitting describes 'Mr Wynn as "A very good gentleman . . . he is very kind to his tenants, and a very good lady is Mrs Wynn, sir; in the winter she gives much soup to the poor."' The Williams Wynns became known as 'the uncrowned kings of north Wales', so vast were their land holdings and so far-reaching their influence. By the nineteenth century the family owned 150,000 acres in Denbighshire, Meirionnydd and Montgomeryshire and it sent representatives for Denbighshire to Parliament from 1716 to 1885. Borrow himself refers to Sir Watkin as 'the Marquis of Carabas of Denbighshire.'

The scenery became wilder as Borrow went on his way. At Pant Paddock he drank gratefully from a little well by the roadside and learnt with excitement that he was near the river Conway. 'One of the great poets of my country calls it the old Conway'. He is referring to Thomas Gray who in 1757 published 'The Last Bard':

> On a rock, whose haughty brow
> Frowns o'er old
> Conway's foaming flood.
> Robed in the sable garb of woe,
> With haggard eyes, the Poete stood;
> Loose his beard and hoary hair
> Stream'd like a meteor
> Through the troubled air.

It is based on the myth, first made popular by Thomas Carte in his *History of England*, that at the time of the conquest Edward I had ordered that all the Welsh bards should be killed to prevent them from transmitting their oral history and culture. The last bard hurls himself to his death rather than submit to such cruel genocide.

Thomas Jones, *The Bard*, 1774. Described by the art historian Peter Lord as 'the definitive interpretation of the subject', it depicts a view of 'Welshness' highly romanticised, yet defiant, proud and free.

As he proceeded towards Betws y Coed, following the course of the Conway, the surroundings became more and more magnificent:

> I was now amidst stupendous hills, whose paps, peaks and pinnacles seemed to rise to the very heaven . . . Coming to the bottom of the pass I crossed over by an ancient bridge, and passing through a small town found myself in a beautiful valley with majestic hills on either side.

He was describing the Vale of Conway which was then a fashionable holiday resort and a retreat, it seems, for students, who would retire there in the summer months to pursue their studies. About three miles beyond Betws y Coed, he was persuaded by a woman at the roadside to go and view the Swallow Falls, which he did, afterwards rewarding his guide with sixpence. Nowadays the falls have been commercialised on a more formal basis and the tourist must pay a fixed fee before passing through a turnstile which gives access to the viewing platforms. The falls themselves, however, if a little crowded, fully justify Borrow's description:

> First there are a number of little foaming torrents, bursting through rocks about twenty yards above the promontory, on which I stood. Then come two beautiful rolls of white water, dashing into a pool a little way above the promontory; then there is a swirl of water round its corner into a pool below on its right, black as death and seemingly of great depth; then a rush through a very narrow outlet into another pool, from which the water clamours away down the glen. Such is the . . . Swallow Fall; called so from the rapidity with which the waters rush along.

Betws y Coed in summer: no longer the ideal retreat for those who seek scholastic seclusion.

Borrow continued on his way stopping first to enquire the name of Moel Siabod and then to inspect a 'monticle', or mound, which stood in a meadow by the river. He was unsure whether this was a natural feature or a man-made burial mound, but he thought it a very suitable resting place for a Celtic king. The mound is at OS 737569 and of natural, probably glacial origin. At Capel Curig he refreshed himself in a smart hotel 'amidst a great deal of fashionable company' whose disdainful looks – he had been walking for twenty miles now on a very hot day – he was able to bear with perfect equanimity.

Borrow now turned north-west at the point where the A5 meets the A4086. After an hour's walking he came to 'a bleak moor, extending for a long way amidst wild sterile hills.' It is curious that he should use the word 'hills' to describe mountains as craggy and impressive as Tryfan. Especially as it is very often the other way round with Borrow; he uses the word 'mountain' for what we would nowadays regard as merely hills. The first of these hills was Gallt yr Ogof adjacent to which Borrow met two wretched and sickly-looking children; cottagers whose parents made a bare living from the hand production of wire-work for fencing. He learns of their illiteracy or near illiteracy – there are no

31

books in the house – and of the harshness and uncertainty of their lives. There are times when the children have no bread, and they are much afflicted by illness, quite possibly the result of malnutrition. The name of the cottage where the children lived was *Helyg*. Borrow comments that he has learnt something of Welsh cottage life from these sickly children, but he is not in general the writer we turn to for information on social conditions. Llangollen had suffered a terrible outbreak of scarlet fever the year before his visit, but there is no mention of this in *Wild Wales*. Described by Borrow as a 'wretched hovel', today *Helyg* is in use as a mountaineer's hut.

The mighty Tryfan and Llyn Ogwen (right).

His next companion occupied a much happier position on the social ladder. He was a carpenter. A cheerful man who accompanied Borrow as far as *Ty'n-y-maes* and who was much amused by the former's ability to speak Welsh. It may be that Borrow was so entertained by the carpenter's company that he neglected to observe the grandeur of the scenery through which he was passing, for he says nothing about the Glyder mountains, although he does mention Llyn Ogwen and a 'gloomy-looking valley' which lay beyond it. On parting from the carpenter, Borrow learns that he is a teetotaller and pays him the accolade of being the only one he had met who did not 'make a parade of his abstinence'. Striding on through the evening- it was past eight o'clock now- he went through Bethesda, a town whose scriptural name, he was informed, was belied by the manners of its people. The people who thronged the town and whose unbiblical manners excited such remark had undoubtedly been attracted there by the slate industry. The population of the Bethedsa district multiplied by three and a half times from 1801 to 1881. He completed the last few miles to Bangor in good-humoured competition with a market gardener who was able to match Borrow's vigorous six-miles-an-hour.

Telford's bridge today and, below, a more westerly view also showing Stephenson's Britannia bridge, 1850 after Hugh Jones

CHAPTER FOUR

Bangor, Beaumaris and Snowdon

Reunited with his family in Bangor, Borrow spent some time strolling about the town with Henrietta. We meet with more Irish people here. On the one hand, a down at heel bookseller who is too proud to beg but not above leaving that kind of work to his wife and daughter. On the other hand, a band of wild-looking men and even wilder-looking women who rush through the street aggressively trying to sell their tin wares. Borrow contrasts the 'free, independent, and almost graceful carriage' of these with the 'poor mean-spirited booktramper'.

They spent some time on the bridges over the Menai Strait. One for ordinary traffic, 'a most beautiful suspension bridge, completed in 1820, the result of the mental and manual labours of the ingenious Telford'. The other, only recently completed, Robert Stephenson's Britannia Tubular bridge for rail traffic, to Borrow 'a wonderful structure . . . but anything but graceful'. His language is notable when he returns to the subject of Telford's bridge in chapter 28. In place of the dry facts of an engineering feat he refers to 'the mighty Telford flinging over the strait an iron suspension bridge'. His

Promenaders on the Menai Bridge in 1850. Lithograph by W. Crane.

imagery at once transforms Telford from industrial genius into a giant or hero from some ancient saga. It is the sort of language for which the term 'Borrovian' was invented.

He returns to the subject of the bridge to introduce and translate lines written by the bard Robert Lleiaf in the early seventeenth century:

> I will go to the land of Mona, notwithstanding the water of the Menai,
> across the sand, without waiting for the ebb.

Remarkable lines which demonstrate the foresight of one who anticipated the building of a bridge over the Straits. But not quite so remarkable as the anonymous englyn of the mid-seventeenth century which he renders as:

I got up in Mona as soon as 'twas light,
At nine in old Chester my breakfast I took;
In Ireland I dined, and in Mona, ere night,
By the turf fire sat, in my own ingle nook.

A truly prophetic verse, he argues, for it foresees not only the building of a bridge, but also the advent of steam railways, which in fact did not link Holyhead and Chester until 1849. Borrow proceeds to a long digression into the nature of the second sight. We shall not follow him there, but cross the Menai Strait instead to visit Beaumaris.

Borrow took the ferry across to Anglesey and then the present A545 to Beaumaris. He went straight to the castle, the last and most ambitious of Edward I's castles in Wales, begun in 1295 but never entirely completed. Borrow's statement that the fortress is 'built on the site of a palace belonging to the ancient kings of North Wales, and a favourite residence of Owain Gwynedd' is at variance with Cadw's information which says that the castle was 'raised on an entirely new site, without earlier buildings to fetter its designer's creative genius'. No one could dispute though the splendours of Beaumaris Bay which Borrow admires in extravagant terms:

'What a bay!' said I, 'for beauty it is superior to the far-famed one of Naples.'

Beaumaris in 1852. An engraving by Alfred Summers shows the ivy-clad castle as a fashionable visiting ground.

Beaumaris Castle. The Gate Next the Sea today and, below, a general view from the north.

The Llanberis path on the right, Borrow and his daughter's route to the summit of Snowdon.

No visit to Snowdonia or *Eryri* can be complete without an ascent to its greatest peak *Yr Wyddfa*, the highest mountain in Wales and England at 3,560 feet. For Borrow, Snowdon's interest lies in its picturesque beauty, in its connections with history, but above all in its connections with romance. A romance derived from Arthurian legend and reinforced by poetic tradition.

To climb Snowdon, Borrow and his family travelled first to Caernarfon where he deals briefly with the town's most notable feature 'The grand old castle . . . built by Edward I after the fall of his brave adversary Llewelyn.' It was here that the future Edward II was born, whom Edward I presented to the Welsh as an infant, promising that their future prince could speak not a word of English. From Caernarfon they continued to Llanberis where a guide was hired for the climb. The Llanberis path is long and laborious but not steep, and is popular today as Borrow observes it was in 1854: 'We were far from being the only visitors to the hill this day.' In his day about 10,000 people a year would reach the summit by its several routes. Nowadays the figure is greater than half a million. Part of this huge increase is accounted for by the passengers carried on the Snowdon Mountain Railway which opened towards the end of the nineteenth century.

Caernarfon Castle from an engraving of the 1860s.

Borrow and his daughter rested briefly in the region of Clogwyn, where the penultimate railway station now stands, before making their final assault on the summit which is the only part of this route which presents much difficulty. Safely arrived at the top Borrow delivers a short harangue to Henrietta on Snowdon's Welsh name,

Yr Wyddfa, which is the mutated form of *gwyddfa* meaning a tumulus and declaims a couple of stanzas of the poetry of Goronwy Owen. The English bystanders on the summit are rather scornful of this poetic outburst, a scorn which Borrow returns declaring his shame in belonging to so materialistic a race as the English, but a Welshman approaches him with interest asking him whether he is a Breton. One conjectures that when Borrow recited Welsh poetry natives of Wales recognised that they were listening to something Celtic, but somehow not quite Welsh.

As the party began to descend from the summit Henrietta, who was a keen botanist, spotted a plant growing from a crag by the side of the path. The guide gallantly sprang forward to collect it for her. The plant is not named. Borrow describes it simply as 'belonging to a species of which [Henrietta] had long been desirous of possessing a specimen', but it is quite likely that this was a Snowdon Lily. If it was, Borrow would have been thrilled to know that the plant's botanical name is *Lloydia serotina*, so-called in honour of its finder Edward Lhuyd whose *Archaeologia Britannica* Borrow had encountered in his youth and whose Celtic journeys probably served as an inspiration for Borrow's own journeys.

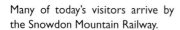
Many of today's visitors arrive by the Snowdon Mountain Railway.

Black and white photograph by Francis Bedford shows the summit of Snowdon in the mid-nineteenth century.

Manifold were the objects which we saw from the brow of Snowdon, but of all the objects which we saw, those which filled us with most delight and admiration, were numerous lakes and lagoons, which, like sheets of ice or polished silver, lay reflecting the rays of the sun in the deep valleys at his feet.

CHAPTER FIVE

Anglesey or Ynys Môn

For Borrow, Anglesey was an island of poets. For him, it did 'not abound in the beauties of nature, but there never was such a place for poets; you meet a poet, or the birthplace of a poet everywhere.' Indeed, his main object in visiting the island was to see the birthplace of Goronwy Owen, whose poetry he had read in his youth.

Finding his way to the bard's former dwelling was no easy feat, but, asking directions before setting out, he accomplished the first part of the journey with relative ease, arriving at the village of Pentraeth and taking refreshment at the hostelry of Hugh Pritchard. Modern pilgrims can follow him, observing the Menai Bridge toll-keeper's instructions and travelling straight into Anglesey until they reach the four crosses cross-roads. There they must take the road to the right, now the main A5025, and pursue its course to Pentraeth. But here they must be warned. The Panton Arms, which looks so obviously like the pub where Borrow drank, is not so at all. In fact he was entertained at the White Horse an establishment across the road, now demolished.

He had some difficulty in making his way from Pentraeth to Goronwy Owen's house or Tafarn Goch and was assisted in doing so by a miller and his family whose simple hospitality he found deeply moving and by a man who mistook him for a Spaniard and began speaking to him in Spanish. The easiest way to get to the poet's house is to take the minor road from Pentraeth to Brynteg, which passes through Llanbedrgoch. Once in Brynteg, turn left in the direction of Llangefni. When Borrow finally reached the poet's birthplace he found it occupied by an elderly woman and her five orphaned grandchildren, distant relatives of Goronwy Owen himself. Borrow persuaded the eldest child to write something for him in his notebook and he tells us she wrote thus:

'Ellen Jones yn perthyn o bell i gronow owen', which is 'Ellen Jones belonging from afar to Gronwy Owen'.

In fact we know from the survival of the notebook that the little girl actually wrote *'Ellen Jones yn pithyn pell i gronow owen'* and Borrow attempted to improve her Welsh by rendering it as he did.

Many years later, in 1910, Ellen Jones, now Ellen Thomas, was sought out and interviewed by George Porter of Denbigh. The episode had made a great impression on her and she had carefully preserved a book from which Borrow had asked her to read to him. Of the stranger himself she recalled that he had the appearance of possessing great strength. He had 'Bright eyes and shabby dress, more like a merchant than a gentleman, or like a man come to buy cattle. But, dear me! He did speak *funny* Welsh, he could not pronounce the 'Ll', and his voice was very high; but perhaps that was because my grandmother was deaf.' He had a good vocabulary, but poor pronunciation.

Ellen Thomas's statement bears out what Borrow himself has to say about his pronunciation of the Welsh letter 'Ll':

> The double l of the Welsh is by no means the terrible guttural which English people generally suppose it to be, being in reality a pretty liquid, exactly resembling in sound the Spanish ll, the sound of which I had mastered before commencing Welsh.

This surely gives us a clue as to why Borrow was mistaken for a Spaniard. The man who thus mistook him had been a sailor, had travelled to Chile and to California, had prospered there and returned to his native Ynys Môn where he was building a house. In the Americas he had learned Spanish. So when Borrow came along with his funny pronunciation and Spanish sounding 'Ll's' it may have seemed only natural to respond to him in that language. The man's name was William Thomas and he has left a memorial to his travels in the name of the house he built which is now the California Inn.

The church at Penmynydd which contains the tomb of Gronw Fychan.

Borrow returned to stay that night at the White Horse in Pentraeth. His experiences remind us that privacy is a relatively modern luxury, and certainly not one to be guaranteed in the more rough and ready hostelry. He found himself in a short bed and sharing his room with two snoring farm labourers. In the scenes at the pub he treats us to two contrasting characters. The drover Mr Bos, all boorish bluster, and Mr Pritchard the publican who has travelled widely as a steamship engineer but who modestly disclaims much knowledge of the world because he has not travelled 'with edification'. For all his pomposity and obnoxious swagger, we must concede that Mr Bos's view of Anglesey – 'I can't conceive how any person, either gentle or simple, could have any business in Anglesey save that business was pigs or cattle'- is much more accurate and realistic than Borrow's view of Anglesey as an island of poets.

From Pentraeth, Borrow headed to Penmynydd, there to visit the church which reputedly held the effigies and the remains of Owain Tudor and his wife Catherine, widow of Henry V. They were the grandparents of Henry Tudor who triumphed at the Battle of Bosworth and founded the Tudor dynasty as Henry VII. Borrow's judgement is that the tomb is doubtless:

> One of the Tudor race, and of a gentle partner of his, but not of the Rose of Mona and Catherine of France. Her bones rest in some corner of Westminster's noble abbey; his moulder . . . where Mortimer's Cross once stood . . . where one of the hardest battles which ever bloodied English soil was fought.

In fact Owain Tudor was captured at the battle of Mortimer's Cross and executed at Hereford, but Borrow is quite right about the tomb in the church. That belongs to Gronw Fychan and his wife and dates from the late fourteenth century.

Not all the poets whom Borrow encountered on Ynys Môn were of such established reputation as Goronwy Owen. The postmaster who had given him directions to Goronwy Owen's house had declared himself to be a poet, though the humblest of the island in his own estimation. Such modesty was not to be found in the mysterious man in grey whom Borrow met at Dyffryn Gaint (probably Caint). This man, who is referred to only by the initials 'J.W.', travels with a sycophantic companion who continually congratulates him for being 'the greatest prydydd (poet) in the world'. Although he makes his living as an innkeeper the calling of bard gives him such prestige that even the local land-owning gentry must treat him with deference and wait patiently upon his muse.

Borrow's treatment of this man is complex but mocking at heart. He leaves the bard, who by this time is becoming quite animated with drink, assuring him that he will patronise the latter's inn at Llangefni. But a few sentences later he makes an apparently innocent, but surely ironic, reference to 'sober poets for

Llangefni today.

which Anglesey has always been so famous'. Whatever Borrow's attitude to his new poet acquaintance, his intention of bringing a bit of business his way by buying a pint and a chop at his hostelry is certainly genuine. Unfortunately Llangefni boasts two establishments called the '- Arms', one a common ale-house kept by the poet, the other a grand hotel which Borrow enters by mistake. The suspicious reader may be forgiven for thinking that the poet deliberately directed Borrow to the wrong house. However, misunderstanding is one of the bases of comedy, and misunderstanding continues when the unspecified pint which Borrow orders turns out to be a pint of sherry. Despite his contempt for the 'silly, sickly compound' he manages to dispatch it with surprising ease!

> 'What detestable stuff!' said I, after I had drunk it. 'However, as I shall have to pay for it I may as well go through with it.' So I poured myself out another glass, and by the time I had finished the chop I had finished the sherry also.

There is more comedy to be extracted from Borrow's conversation with the curtseying, respectable but slightly disdainful waitress. Still labouring under the misapprehension that he is in the poet's house, Borrow inquires of her:

'Has your master written any poetry lately?'

'Sir!' said the damsel, staring at me.

'Any poetry,' said I,' any pennillion?'

'No, sir,' said the damsel: 'my master is a respectable man, and would scorn to do anything of the kind.'

Borrow has a great talent for dialogue and one can almost hear these lines being spoken on stage.

Having completed his meal, Borrow restored friendly relations with the waitress by means of an ample tip and set off for Caergybi or Holyhead. He followed the route of the old A5 which is now the B5109. At a house called *Gwyn dy* he reports a conversation with two men, one of whom protests that 'the lands are almost entirely taken possession of by Saxons', a complaint which has a current political resonance.

At Holyhead, Borrow swallowed his prejudice against railways – the memories of short beds and snoring companions were all too recent – and put up at the Railway Hotel, a building which survived until 1978 when it was finally pulled down. Here he met yet another poet in the form of the hotel boots, a grey-haired, venerable-looking man who conversed with him of Goronwy Owen and Lewis Morris.

On the harbour side at Caergybi, Borrow describes a little adventure. Two or three dozen reapers were hanging about: Irishmen waiting for their boat to come in. They had rather a ruffianly look and all of them were armed with cudgels. These men mistook him for a priest, the Catholic priest Father Toban – a recurrence of the theme that we first encountered in Chester – and threatened to give him a beating unless he gave them a blessing. Never unequal to the unusual situation, Borrow summoned up 'the best Latin blessing [he] could remember', which he 'had got by memory out of an old Popish book of devotion' that he had bought in his boyhood. It is quite likely that this whole incident is fabricated. Certainly there is no clue to it in the notes he made in his diary:

Saw Irish reapers lying asleep on shady side of breakwater – fisherboats boys bathing – turned back more Irish reapers sleeping under stone wall some talking Irish – middle sized well made fellows with something of a ruffianly look – shillalahs in the hands of some – stared at me.

When Borrow presented the first draft of *Wild Wales* to his publisher, John Murray, the latter had praised it for its style of English, but lamented the lack of 'stirring incident' in it which he feared would prevent it from being commercially successful. Perhaps then the scene with the reapers is an example of a fictionalised 'stirring incident' later inserted by Borrow.

Looking south-east from Holyhead Mountain, across Malltraeth Bay and the Menai Strait.

Holyhead Mountain, site of the ancient hillfort Caer y Tŵr.

Taking the advice of the hotel boots, Borrow swallowed for a second time his prejudice against railways and returned to Bangor by train, but not before he had ascended the head under the guidance of the boots' nephew. There, above the lighthouse at South Stack, he stood on the cairn at the summit of Holyhead Mountain.

> The prospect, on every side, was noble: the blue interminable sea to the west and north; the whole stretch of Mona to the east; and far away to the south the mountainous region of Eryri, comprising some of the most romantic hills in the world.

A far cry from the hotel back at Bangor which he found populated by weekend holidaymakers from Liverpool and Manchester, to Borrow 'the scum of manufacturing England'.

CHAPTER SIX

Bangor to Bala

Borrow describes the road from Bangor to Caernarfon as very good and the scenery interesting. He made one stop along the way at Portdinorwic or Felinheli. There he fell into conversation with a group of seafaring men who were debating the existence of a sea serpent, perhaps the conger eel which inhabits much of the waters around Wales. When Borrow questions the men about the name of the village, which he interprets as 'Port of the Norway man', deriving from piratical Danes and Norse of old, the men have nothing to say, but they tell Borrow about the nearby quarrying of slate and its export from the harbour. Another example of how Borrow's interests are rooted so much more in legends and the past than they are in the modern industrial Wales which he found emerging before him. He mentions the slate trade, but only in passing. He seems more at home somehow with sea monsters and Danes of old.

He had dealt with Caernarfon Castle in his earlier chapter on Snowdon and so on his second visit he forsook the castle in favour of the Castle Inn, which fronts the square adjacent to the castle as he describes. He did not stay in the town but left at three o'clock for Beddgelert. It was a Sunday and this prompted him to stop at Croesywaun to attend part of a church service. Such devotion was not a

An immense mountain . . . just like a couchant elephant.

foregone conclusion with him. While staying at Llangollen his wife Mary wrote to her mother-in-law reassuring her that her son was 'very regular in his morning and evening devotions, so that we all have abundant cause for thankfulness'.

He left the village heading south-east along the A4085. He mentions Mount Eilio, more properly Moel Eilio, but the 'immense mountain' lying over against it on the south 'just like a couchant elephant', must surely be Mynydd Mawr and Craig Cwmbychan, not Pen Drws Coed as he has it. It is thought that Borrow walked without either maps or guide book although both would have been available to him, so the degree of accuracy he does achieve is really quite astonishing, especially as he did not usually make more than sketchy notes and some time elapsed between his journeys and the writing of *Wild Wales*. When he came to the bridge over the Afon Gwyrfai near to Betws Garmon he stood enraptured by the scenery:

> As I stood upon that bridge I almost fancied myself in paradise; everything looked so beautiful or grand – green, sunny meadows lay all around me, intersected by the brook, the waters of which ran with tinkling laughter over a shingly bottom. Noble Eilio to the north; enormous Pen Drws Coed to the south; a tall mountain far beyond them to the east. 'I never was in such a lovely spot!'

He stopped for ale, probably in Betws Garmon and here he found the people of the house kept a dog called Perro, a Spanish name which set Borrow to musing on its possible origins. The landlord's stolid logic in response to Borrow's question is superb:

> 'Perro!' said I; 'why do you call the dog Perro?'
> 'We call him Perro,' said the man, 'because his name is Perro'.

What an eccentric figure Borrow so often must have cut. Here he was in a little Snowdonia tavern, pondering questions of word origin and banging his fist on the table with vexation. No wonder the locals whispered about him in Welsh, thinking he wouldn't be able to understand them. Jan Morris informs us in her book *Wales* that shipwrecked survivors of the Spanish Armada are said to have settled in Gwynedd, and that this, in fable at any rate, accounts for farm dogs in the region often being called Perro.

The Snowdon Ranger's house, now in use as a youth hostel.

After leaving the inn, Borrow passed a little mill by the side of Afon Gwyrfai and eventually reached Llyn Cwellyn. On the shores of the lake, he fell into conversation with two men, one the Snowdon Ranger, the other his son-in-law, a slate miner. The conversation of the slate miner gives us some little insight into the lives of these workers. Quarrymen would often live in barracks during the working week and walk long distances on Saturday nights to be with their families on Sunday. This went on within living memory. A 75 year old man, retired and returned to his birthplace of Beddgelert, recalls how in his childhood quarrymen would *run* all the way from the mines at Blaenau Ffestiniog to their homes and families in Beddgelert after the Saturday morning shift, only to do the return journey, somewhat less enthusiastically, on Sunday evening in readiness for another gruelling week's work. The conversation with the old ranger starts rather coldly but seems to thaw as it goes on, with Borrow promising that if he ever climbs the Wyddfa again he will do so under the ranger's guidance, and the ranger eventually concluding that he never saw a nicer gentleman. The ranger too reveals something of his working life, confiding that far too many people for his liking make the ascent from inferior starting points like 'that trumpery place Beth Gelert'. The Ranger's House still stands and is now a youth hostel.

Borrow can hardly tear himself away from the sight of the lake, 'The silver lake and the shadowy mountain'. It is now evening and 'delightfully cool in this land of wonder', but eventually he does so and as he speeds up so too does his prose until he seems to be just jotting down notes directly from his notebook, the frequency of his steps matched by urgent staccato sentences.

Llyn Cwellyn in evening light.

At Beth Gelert or Beddgelert, Borrow put up at the Goat Hotel, 'Large and commodious', but grotesquely populated by characters whom he sketches with vehemence and not a little loathing. There are two military men, one of them 'a tallish fellow' who 'affects the airs of a languishing girl', the other a 'short spuddy fellow' who talks very consequentially about 'the service' when not directing *double entendres* at the decidedly overweight serving girl. The father of the spuddy fellow is present too and he applauds his son's coarse remarks. A fourth character would 'require the pencil of a Hogarth' to do justice to his appearance. 'His countenance is cadaverous', he is dressed 'in a style of superfine gentility' and his conversation sounds most unappealing being 'chiefly about his bile and his secretions'. Odious though these people may have been, Borrow's disgust with them is at least in part conditioned by their discussions on one of the infamous military and legal cases of the day. He concludes this short chapter with:

The Goat Hotel at Beddgelert.

> The spuddy, broad-faced military puppy with spectacles was vociferating to the languishing military puppy, and to his old simpleton of a father, who was listening to him with his usual look of undisguised admiration, about the absolute necessity of kicking Lieutenant P- out of the army for having disgraced 'the service'. Poor P-, whose only crime was trying to defend himself with fist and candlestick from the manual attacks of his brutal messmates.

He is referring to the case of Lieutenant James Edward Perry who was court martialled when he defended himself against the bullying of his fellow officers. *The Times* thundered against Perry's dismissal as 'an act of foul and crying injustice'. Borrow was particularly incensed by the case because Perry was the son of a sergeant and his humble origins had aroused the snobbish resentment of his comrades. Borrow's father too had been a sergeant who rose through the ranks to his captaincy. It was precisely this sort of class prejudice that Borrow rails against as 'gentility nonsense'.

The Crimean War was in progress during the time of Borrow's Welsh tour and occasionally news of the conflict intrudes upon his narrative. When it does so, his attitude to the conduct of the war is sometimes coloured by his views on the case of Lieutenant Perry. In Chapter 56, for example, when news is brought to

Llangollen that Sebastopol has been taken, and then it transpires that an 'interminable siege' has set in and the British have suffered disasters and disgraces – the Charge of the Light Brigade – Borrow comments

> It was quite right and consistent with the justice of God that the British arms should be subjected to disaster and ignominy about that period. A deed of infamous injustice and cruelty had been perpetrated.

He is referring to the case of poor Lieutenant Perry.

Borrow relates for us the legend of the faithful dog Gelert, another case of summary injustice, which was already well known at that time, as indeed it had been since early in the century when David Prichard, manager of the Goat Hotel had begun to broadcast it. Prichard had energetically cultivated the legend as a means of attracting custom to his hotel, and in fact at one time a path led straight from the hotel garden to the site of the supposed grave. Who though, even armed with the knowledge of this commercial manipulation can resist Borrow's verdict: 'Poor Gelert'.

Borrow is full of praise for the scenery around Beddgelert: 'Truly, the valley of Gelert is a wondrous valley – rivalling for grandeur and beauty any vale either in the Alps or Pyrenees.'

His comment is not simply the judgement of a well-travelled man. It also hints at how Welsh scenery, especially the mountainous scenery of Snowdonia was 'discovered' by wealthy English travellers in the later-eighteenth century. When the Revolutionary and Napoleonic Wars began to impede travel on the continent, tourists turned their attention to scenic delights nearer to home. The Aber Glaslyn Valley became particularly well known.

The legend of Gelert.

Presently I came to a bridge bestriding the stream, which a man told me was called Pont Aber Glas Lyn.

There was the rich forest scenery to the north, behind it were the rocks and behind the rocks rose the wonderful conical hill impaling heaven.

Borrow crossed Pont Aber Glaslyn following the road which is now the A4085. Stopping to ask questions of a 'man of open countenance' he learned the names of two mountains. Cnicht, spelt with a 'c' not a 'k', 'a wonderful conical hill impaling heaven', and the Great Hill or Moelwyn Mawr, 'a huge lumpish hill'. He also discovered in his informant a remarkable attribute: here was a tenant farmer who thoroughly approved of his landlord. At a turn of the road he encountered a small neat cottage with a board over the door inscribed 'Tea made here, the draught which cheers but not inebriates'. The cottage was a temperance house, but its occupant was not as high-principled as the magistrates who had refused her a brewing licence, for when Borrow declined her tea she produced a bottle of moonshine whisky, prompting Borrow to 'Those who wish for either whisky or brandy far above proof should always go to a temperance house'. Not entirely a compliment, hinting as it does of double standards! At OS 618428 where the A4085 bends sharply to the right you can still find a small neat cottage, in fact a row of them, but until recently one of them bore a faded board marked 'Tan Lan Café', a reminder of its former tea (and hooch!) serving days.

Just at the turn of the road stood a small neat cottage.

There is another sign at the end of the row of cottages marked 'public footpath' and it must have been this path which Borrow took to lose his way and wander about 'for nearly two hours amidst rocks, thickets, and precipices'. Eventually, however, he found his way onto the B4410, 'a smooth royal road', which took him to Maentwrog. There he restored his depleted energies with brandy and water in the Grapes Inn and fell into discussion with a fellow customer; a discussion which soon took a religious turn. The argument centred on the question of predestination for his gloomy companion was a Calvinist who considered himself irrevocably condemned to eternal damnation. Borrow is much more palatable when he deals with Nonconformist religion than he is when dealing with Catholicism and this scene in the pub is most enjoyable. It is not only his dialogue that has strength; his reported speech too can be very effective. His short, swift, repetitious sentences convey the to-and-fro of the dispute and the unwillingness of either party to give way:

The Grapes Inn at Maentwrog.

> I asked him on what ground he imagined he should be lost; he replied on the ground of being predestined to be lost. I asked him how he knew he was predestined to be lost; whereupon he asked me how I knew I was to be saved; I told him I did not know I was to be saved, but trusted I should be so by belief in Christ . . .

A young lady watercolourist, staying on holiday in Barmouth, painted these pictures of Ffestiniog in 1855. To the right, a present day photograph from the same point of view as below.

Borrow reserves for himself the parting shot but the reader cannot help smiling with him as he leaves his pessimistic companion,

> Looking very miserable, perhaps at finding that he was not quite so certain of eternal damnation as he had hitherto supposed. There can be no doubt that the idea of damnation is anything but disagreeable to some people; it gives them a kind of gloomy consequence in their own eyes. We must be something particular they think, or God would hardly deem it worth His while to torment us for ever.

Borrow retraced his steps a bit to regain the road to Ffestiniog, now the A496. As he travelled his 'mind was full of enthusiastic fancies' concerning the bard Rhys Goch, a partisan of Owain Glyndŵr who is said to have been born in this region and who flourished from the late fourteenth to the mid-fifteenth century. In particular, Borrow was anxious to discover the whereabouts of a stone chair, part of a druidic circle, in which the poet was reputed to have composed his verses. An old man he met along the way could not, or would not tell him anything, being more anxious to hear from an Englishman news from London and the court. Nor did the landlady at the hotel in Ffestiniog know anything of Rhys Goch or his chair. A stroller he met in the square in front of the church could not recall anything definite, though he was full of information about the hotel landlady's tendency to undercharge her guests. The next morning Borrow left the village disappointed both in the matter of Rhys Goch and his chair and in the matter of the hotel bill for that turned out to be a little more than he usually paid.

The old drovers' bridge which crosses afon Taihirion.

He left Ffestiniog by the B4391 and, crossing wild and barren country relieved by the sight of a fresh green valley to the south, eventually came to a wild moor. 'Nothing could be conceived more cheerless than the scenery around' him. The ground was mossy and rushy. There were no houses, only the occasional peat stack and nothing living to be seen except a few sheep. Even today the tarmac road and the modern march of pylons have done little to alter the essential bleakness of this landscape. A glimpse of water diverted him, and finding his way to a small lake which may have been Llyn Tryweryn, but which could also have been Llyn Cors y Barcud, he fell to musing, pondering on the water monster, the *afanc*. This is one of his recurrent interests in *Wild Wales*. We will find him asking questions about it at Dinas Mawddwy and at Strata Florida too. Properly speaking the *afanc* is a beaver and *llostlydan,* the word which Borrow gives, is equally translated as 'beaver'; but in legend *Yr Afanc* is a much more fearsome creature. The Welsh Triads refer to a great water monster which inhabits a bottomless lake, emerging occasionally to cause the inundation of the land around. It was only by the mighty deeds of Hu Gadarn that this monster was quelled. Borrow's analysis – that the crocodilian monster of old gave way to the beaver, which itself is now extinct in Britain – is quite scientific and up to the minute, referring as it does to Victorian discoveries of fossil remains. Borrow's approach is certainly very different from that of his earliest literary hero, Daniel Defoe who dismissed Welsh water legends with: 'They have a great many… fables, not worth relating'.

On regaining the road, Borrow came upon a stream crossed by two bridges, 'one immensely old and terribly dilapidated, the other old enough, but in better repair'. Nearby was an ancient long-house, one of the traditional buildings of Wales, where a hospitable woman gave him water and milk. There is no trace of the long-house now, but there is an old drovers' bridge which survives alongside and to the left of the metalled road, and the house or houses are preserved in name by the stream which is called Afon Taihirion. There is no trace either of the alehouse at Rhyd y fen, where he stopped to drink beer and converse with a farmer on the subject of grain prices, but its name is preserved by the bridge over Afon Tryweryn which is called Pont Rhyd-y-fen. Nor is there any trace of the 'beautiful valley' a little beyond the 'village of the tollgate':

> On my right was a river the farther bank of which was fringed with trees; on my left was a gentle ascent, the lower part of which was covered with yellow luxuriant corn; a little farther on was a green grove, behind which rose up a moel. A more bewitching scene I never beheld.

For this is now beneath Llyn Celyn, the artificial lake which in the 1960s deluged the valley, and the hamlet of Capel Celyn along with it, to make a reservoir to supply Liverpool with water. If it is preserved, it is in Welsh

Llyn Celyn

resentment; it is in the graffiti *'Cofiwch Dryweryn'* (Remember Tryweryn) which one still sees painted here and there on rocks and walls; it is in lines of poetry like R.S. Thomas's 'There are places in Wales I don't go'. One can only wonder at what Borrow would have thought of it all.

In the evening Borrow arrived at Bala in the enjoyable company of a horse dealer who showed him the way to the White Lion. Here we meet the estimable Tom Jenkins, one of the best characters in the book. He is the waiter, but he has the bearing of the master of the house. He has the air, the manner, even the accent of a Frenchman though he is entirely a native of Bala. So much so that he cannot bring himself to admit to anything good about Llangollen. In scenery, in points of interest, even in the ability to brew ale, Llangollen is a 'trumpery hole' in comparison to Bala. But it is the people of Llangollen for whom Jenkins reserves his especial disdain, for they are all drunkards.

> '. . . and nobody can live among them without being a drunkard. There was my nephew-' 'What of him?' said I
>
> 'Why, he went to Llangollen, your honour, and died of a drunken fever in less than a month.'
>
> 'Well, but might he not have died of the same if he had remained at home?'
>
> 'No, your honour, no! he lived here many a year, and never died of a drunken fever; he was rather fond of liquor, it is true, but he never died at

Bala of a drunken fever; but when he went to Langollen he did. Now, your honour, if there is not something more drunken about Llangollen than Bala, why did my nephew die at Llangollen of a drunken fever?'

'Really', said I, 'you are such a close reasoner, that I do not like to dispute with you'.

His logic is impeccable; it is only perhaps in his lateral thinking that he is somewhat adrift!

The White Lion where Borrow stayed in Bala.

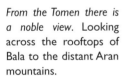

From the Tomen there is a noble view. Looking across the rooftops of Bala to the distant Aran mountains.

Tom Jenkins's ale, which he brewed himself, was equal to the best that Borrow had ever drunk, 'rich and mellow, with scarcely any smack of the hop in it, and though so pale and delicate to the eye nearly as strong as brandy'. Dinner too was excellent, consisting of many more items than he had ordered, but the meal not to be missed at Bala is breakfast:

A noble breakfast it was . . . There was tea and coffee, a goodly white loaf and butter; there were a couple of eggs and two mutton chops. There was broiled and pickled salmon – there was fried trout – there were also potted trout and potted shrimps.

One of the wonders of Bala is the Tomen Bala, a mound of about thirty feet in height and about fifty feet in diameter at the top, much the same size and shape as Glyndŵr's Mount. Borrow says that

Both belong to that brotherhood of artificial mounds of unknown antiquity, found scattered, here and there, throughout Europe and the greater part of Asia . . . [They] seem to have been originally intended as places of sepulture, but in many instances were afterwards used as strongholds, bonhills or beacon-heights, or as places on which adoration was paid to the host of heaven.

The Tomen, Bala.

The origin of the Tomen is still something of a mystery. As Tom Jenkins puts it, 'the Tomen Bala has puzzled many a head'. Rhys Tudur in his *Looking at Bala* suggests that it was a Norman motte and that there was at one time a wooden tower on top. Others suggest a Roman origin. Attempts to find burial remains by excavation have so far been unsuccessful. Interestingly, there are two similar mounds in the neighbourhood, one near Mwnwgl y Llyn (Neck of the lake) and the other called Tomen y Castell (Castle Mound) about a mile and a half to the east.

From Bala, Borrow walked back via Llandrillo and Corwen to rejoin his family in Llangollen. He arrived there on 6 September having spent eleven days on the road and having travelled on foot something like one hundred and forty miles.

Llyn Tegid, or Bala Lake.

CHAPTER SEVEN

Return to Llangollen

The Borrows now spent a further twenty days at Llangollen before Mary and Henrietta returned home and Borrow departed for South Wales. Borrow describes only one family outing during this time, an excursion to Chirk Castle or *Castell y Waun*.

He and his wife and stepdaughter, together with John Jones, walked over the hills, probably passing *Tyn Dŵr* Farm and taking what is now *Llwybr Ceiriog* or the Ceiriog trail. The castle is today in the care of the National Trust and open to visitors, but tours were in those days conducted by the housekeeper. During the 1840s the architect A.W. Pugin had been employed on the castle and the Borrows must have viewed the results of his work. He had refaced the east range and 'gothicised' much of the interior. His colour schemes, and those of his decorator John Crace, were decidedly gaudy. For example, the walls of the saloon were bright green and gold and its ceiling bright blue. His wallpaper for the drawing room was 'crimson plush'. Furnishings were correspondingly rich. The Borrows obviously approved. George comments, 'When we left the castle we all said, not excepting John Jones, that we had never seen in our lives anything more princely and delightful than the interior.' The reaction of the Shrewsbury Archaeological Institute who visited a year later was quite different. They were horrified by the decoration of the saloon and said as much in an article which appeared in *The Builder* in August 1855.

The present day visitor will look in vain for some of the portraits Borrow mentions. In the drawing room for instance there were at one time more than forty paintings, many more than today. It is difficult to be quite certain of his accuracy, but sometimes he gets things wrong because attributions have changed over the years and even the identities of sitters have been rethought. For example, there are no portraits of Nell Gwynne by Peter Lely, but there is a *Portrait of a Courtesan* in the manner of Sir Peter Lely and four further portraits after him depicting other mistresses of Charles II, two of them showing Barbara Villiers. In the long gallery the 'cabinet of ebony and silver presented by Charles the Second to the brave warrior Sir Thomas' can still be seen. Another item that impressed Borrow was 'the huge skin of a lion stretched out upon the floor'. This can be made out quite clearly in a watercolour of the long gallery painted by Lady Hester Leeke in the 1840s and in a photograph taken around 1900.

Chirk Castle from the gardens.

Outside in the castle grounds John Jones led the party down an avenue on the eastern side of the castle to see the figure of a giant. It turned out to be a statue of Hercules, much overgrown then amidst heather and gorse, but now rescued and standing on a grassy fairway in the middle of a lime avenue so that it can be clearly viewed from the castle gardens. When the statue was moved to its present position in 1983 it had become so overgrown that a helicopter was needed to drag it out.

On their return to Llangollen, John Jones took the Borrows by the low road so that they could see the castle lodge and its gates which were considered to be amongst the wonders of Wales. The gates were made from 1712-19 by Robert and John Davies. In the middle of the nineteenth century they would have been standing between the classical

The statue of Hercules.

lodges which were built for them by Joseph Turner at the present visitors' exit. They were moved to the position they now occupy in 1888. Borrow's verdict was that 'the lodge had nothing remarkable in its appearance, but the gate which was of iron was truly magnificent'. Indeed they have more recently been praised as 'the finest achievements of Baroque ironwork in the country'. The wolves which surmount them refer as he says to Ririd Flaidd, a lord of Meirionnydd who died at the beginning of the thirteenth century and from whom the Myddletons of Chirk trace their descent.

The gates of Chirk.

No account of Llangollen can be complete without a mention of the Ladies of Llangollen, Lady Eleanor Butler and Miss Sarah Ponsonby. They were high-born women of Anglo-Irish descent who eloped from their homes and settled in Llangollen in 1778. In 1780 they moved into Plas Newydd and remained there until their respective deaths in 1829 and 1831. During their time there, Borrow was informed, 'the ladies were in the habit of receiving the very first people in Britain.' Their notable visitors included Edmund Burke, Humphry Davy, Mrs Piozzi (formerly Mrs Thrale, Doctor Johnson's friend), Richard Sheridan, Robert Southey, Josiah Wedgwood and the Duke of Wellington.

William Wordsworth too was a visitor. He sent the ladies a sonnet composed in the grounds of Plas Newydd and it was said by a later owner that he offended them by referring to their house as 'a low roofed cot'. They didn't think much of his poetry either. Borrow describes the house as 'a small gloomy mansion',

Plas Newydd today with Castell Dinas Brân looming in the background.

while a guide book of 1856, only two years after his visit remarked that it was 'fantastical rather than tasteful'. The heavily ornamented porch and window canopies were in place in the ladies' time but the house would certainly not have had the striking 'mock-Tudor' appearance that we see today. A later owner, General Yorke who bought the house in 1876, was responsible for that.

Lady Eleanor and Miss Ponsonby were generally popular with the people of Llangollen. Indeed John Jones refers to their charity. He also mentions the auction which took place after their deaths:

> . . . a grand auction it was and lasted four days. Oh, what a throng of people there was, some of whom came from a great distance, to buy the curious things, of which there were plenty.

In fact the auction lasted for seven days in August 1832. One of the many curious things included for sale was a lock of Mary Queen of Scots's hair. The 1832 Sales Catalogue has survived and has proved a valuable document for researchers who seek to restore the interior to the state it was in at the time of the Ladies.

During Borrow's second stay at Llangollen, there were no great pilgrimages in search of the graves of poets, but he does tell us that he bought a book in the market called *Y Llwyn Celyn* or the *Holly Grove* which contained the life of Twm o'r Nant, or Thomas Edwards, the poet whose portrait he had been shown at Valle Crucis Abbey. Borrow gives us a long account of Twm o'r Nant's life together with a lengthy extract from one of his interludes on *Riches and Poverty*. He tells us that the interlude grew out of the medieval morality play, itself a product of the mystery play. However, morality was not the only purpose of the interlude; it could also be used as a means of attacking the social order through satire. Landowners, lawyers, bailiffs and clergymen were all legitimate targets. This is why Borrow's acquaintance, the church clerk, stresses that Tom was 'very satirical and very clever'. Indeed his whole household was very satirical and clever and 'it was impossible to live with Twm o'r Nant without learning to be clever and satirical'. Another of Borrow's acquaintances at Llangollen gives us a clue to the other feature of the interlude: its ribaldry. The Baptist coal seller whom he calls Smollett's Morgan declares:

> There never yet was a writer of Interludes, or a person who went about playing them, that was not a scamp . . . No Baptist connection would ever have a writer of Interludes in it, not Twm o'r Nant himself, unless he left his ales and Interludes and wanton hussies, for the three things are sure to go together.

Part of the popular appeal of the interlude lay in its sexual suggestiveness, for in condemning moral laxity the players would at the same time describe it in lurid terms. The interlude, as Borrow puts it, 'yielded to the influence of Methodism' and it was in fact its licentiousness that led to the increasing disapproval of the Nonconformists from the late eighteenth century.

For all that Borrow devotes a chapter to *Riches and Poverty*, his judgement is that Twm o'r Nant 'was greater as a man than a poet, and his fame depends more on the cleverness, courage and energy . . . that he possessed than on his interludes'.

Twm o'r Nant.
Oil on canvas, 1763.

Borrow made one long expedition on foot during this time and that was to Wrexham, partly to explore the hill road to the town but also to buy a book that had just been published on Welsh Methodism. He probably went by way of Rock Farm, Tŷ Newydd and Plas Yn Eglwyseg. We can locate him fairly exactly at Craig y Forwyn which is at OS 234 479, 'an enormous crag of a strange form rising to the very heavens, the upper part of it a dull white colour'. He spoke to a man in the region of this rock near a house which is named as Plas Uchaf, Upper Mansion. That is no longer marked on the map but it may have been the manor house at OS 228 479. Plas Isaf, the lower house, has gone too, but the middle house Tŷ Canol can still be found at OS 222 475. About half a mile further on he went wrong, taking a path to the east and then striking out across the bare hillside to the north-east. He eventually found his way to Cadwgan Hall at OS 299 487. From there it was only half an hour at his best pace to reach Wrexham. The walker of today can avoid Borrow's problems by remaining on the path which runs north from Craig y Forwyn. That is Offa's Dyke path which winds its way past Hafod Farm to emerge at New Brighton and Minera.

At Wrexham, Borrow bought his book on Methodism, possibly *Welsh Methodism* by John Hughes, a weighty volume which lent respectability to his rather mud-splashed appearance in the dining room of the Wynnstay Arms. At dinner he was warned of the dangers of returning to Llangollen on foot by the common road, for it was Saturday night and the miners would all be in the pubs getting drunk. His response is typically robust:

> 'If not more than two attack me,' said I, 'I shan't much mind. With this book I am sure I can knock down one, and I think I can find fair play for the other with my fists'.

Fortunately such extreme measures were not necessary, but he gives us a glimpse of the riotous way in which the miners used to compensate for the rigours and hardships of a long working week. Just outside Wrexham he passed a red public house, from which issued 'a scream of Welsh'. Not the place for a Saxon, he thought, unless they were spoiling for a fight. At Rhiwabon too there was 'a prodigious noise' in the pubs, the sound of colliers carousing.

Borrow gives us a number of sketches of life in old Llangollen. Among these is his description of the market in Chapters 22 and 58. The market was then held in a square somewhat to the south-east of the church. Country people would come to town with young pigs and the townsfolk would buy them to take home. There they would be kept in a shed in the backyard and fattened for eventual slaughter, a much needed addition to the family diet. Larger animals though would attract the attention of the livestock dealers from England, 'the gents from Wolverhampton'. From Borrow's portrayal of these, albeit seen in a dream, we can assume that they prospered at their trade:

Methought I was in Llangollen fair in the place where the pigs were sold, in the midst of Welsh drovers, immense hogs and immense men whom I took to be the gents of Wolverhampton. What huge fellows they were! almost as huge as the hogs for which they higgled; the generality of them dressed in brown sporting coats, drab breeches, yellow-topped boots, splashed all over with mud, and with low-crowned broad-brimmed hats. One enormous fellow particularly caught my notice. I guessed he must have weighed at least eleven score, he had a half-ruddy, half-tallowy face, brown hair and thin whiskers.

We are introduced too, to some of the inhabitants of the town. For example, the venerable old Mr Jones, provision dealer and general merchant who had formerly been the church clerk. His premises were in Bridge Street on the left as you go towards the church. There are a number of eighteenth-century buildings along here and even today the shops and businesses have an attractive old-fashioned quality. Then there is the mysteriously unnamed A-, the innkeeper whom John Jones thought 'the clebberest man in Llangollen'. He had spent his former days as servant to a travelling gentleman, had five times crossed the Alps and been in every capital of Europe. He kept the pub which immediately confronts you as you cross the bridge to the north. A little out of the town, along the river bank to the west we meet the man who put Borrow so much in mind of Morgan in Tobias Smollett's *Roderick Random*, the Baptist coal merchant who so righteously disapproves of interludes. Borrow pokes gentle fun at this man and his religion.

The colourful Bridge Street where old Mr Jones had his premises.

I asked him in what line of business he was, he told me that he sold coals. From his complexion and the hue of his shirt, I had already concluded that he was in some grimy trade. I then inquired of what religion he was, and received for answer that he was a Baptist. I thought that both himself and part of his apparel would look all the better for a good immersion.

But he redresses the balance in Chapter 19, admitting that he got rather the worse of it in a discussion on baptism. While he rarely gives way in his anti-Catholicism, Borrow is much less intransigent in his dealings with other Christian sects.

Towards the end of October, the holiday at an end, the Borrows began to make arrangements to leave Llangollen, Mary and Henrietta to return home and George to join them after a walking tour into south Wales. For Borrow preparations were relatively simple:

I bought a small leather satchel with a lock and key, in which I placed a white linen shirt, a pair of worsted stockings, a razor and a prayer-book. Along with it I bought a leather strap with which to sling it over my shoulder; I got my boots new soled, my umbrella, which was rather dilapidated, mended; put twenty sovereigns into my purse, and then said I am all right for the Deheubarth. [The South]

Llangollen in summer, today.

CHAPTER EIGHT

The Journey to South Wales

On 21 October, Borrow said goodbye to Mary and Henrietta at Plas Newydd and set out to climb the southern hill from Llangollen for the last time. There lay the town beneath him

> With its chimneys placidly smoking, its pretty church rising in its centre, its blue river dividing it into two nearly equal parts, and the mighty hill of Brennus, overhanging it from the north.

He sighed and, repeating verses of Einion Du, turned away over the top of the hill. He was twice more to visit Wales, but he never returned to Llangollen. At first he passed through familiar country, Glyn Ceiriog and Pont y Meibion. At Tregeiriog he stopped on the bridge to admire a painterly scene of rural life with pigs browsing in front of a water mill. Following the course of the Ceiriog, he reached Llanarmon and there he stopped for ale. In the pub there was a man staring at a Welsh newspaper. He could not read, but hoped that by staring at the letters he might in time be able to decipher them. Borrow's advice is to attend evening classes.

The Wynnstay Arms at Llanrhaeadr-ym-Mochnant.

With some difficulty resulting from confusing directions and boggy tracks, Borrow made the rest of his way to Llanrhaeadr-ym-Mochnant. He was directed to the Wynnstay Arms which he describes as large but not very cheerful. He was the only guest at the hotel except for a rowdy man in the kitchen whom the landlady dubbed 'a low Englishman'. Of the town itself he says 'Llan Rhyadr is a small place, having nothing remarkable in it save an ancient church and a strange little antique market-house, standing on pillars'. Later he was to view the church in the company of the church clerk, 'a middle-aged man of a remarkably intelligent countenance'. The clerk informed Borrow that the church had been built in the sixteenth century and that among its

Llanrhaeadr then and now. Borrow's strange little antique market-house is long gone, but the building that today houses the Spar looks much as it did in John Thomas's photograph of the late-nineteenth century.

remarkable vicars it boasted Doctor William Morgan, Doctor Robert South and Walter D-. This last whom Borrow never fully names was Walter Davies or Gwallter Mechain who held the living at Llanrhaeadr from 1807 to 1849. He was a poet and editor of Welsh manuscripts. The importance of William Morgan cannot be overlooked for he was the first to translate the Bible into Welsh. He is remembered by a plaque on the church gate.

Title page of William Morgan's Bible (1588). William Morgan (1545-1604) entered the living of Llanrhaeadr-ym-Mochnant in 1578 and it was here, and for a time in London, that he translated the Bible into Welsh, an achievement of immense importance. His work not only brought the word of God to the Welsh people in their own language, but also had far-reaching literary, linguistic and cultural consequences. As the *New Companion to Welsh Literature* puts it: it was 'the foundation and example for all the literature written in Wales after the end of the sixteenth century and it helped to create a consciousness of national identity over the centuries which followed.'

Borrow's principal object in being at Llanrhaeadr was the town's proximity to Sycharth or Sychnant, the headquarters of Owain Glyndŵr. Accordingly, having inquired directions of the hotel cook, he set out on the road to Llangedwyn, now the B4396. Along the way he met a young couple from Wrexham, English basket sellers with whom he fell into conversation. The couple scandalise Borrow by intimating that their only interests in life are beer and sex and he leaves them reflecting that the people of Wrexham are the worst people in Wales. There is no indication from Borrow's diary that this conversation ever took place. His notes offer only the following bland record:

> I overtook two people a man and a woman laden with baskets which hung around them on every side – the man was a young fellow about twenty-eight with a round face fair flaxen hair and rings in his ears – spoke to them – asked whether they were English. The man said they were asked them where they came from – Wrexham.

We have seen how in *Wild Wales* Borrow is inclined to dismiss his own race, the Saxons, as 'coarse-hearted sensual and selfish'. Whether he invented this conversation to emphasise this view of them, or whether it really took place, we have no way of knowing.

Travelling on, Borrow turned left at Llangedwyn and was escorted to Glyndŵr's hill by a cottager who lived near the Sycharth factory. He sat down on the brow of the hill and there tried to recall Glyndŵr 'and the times that are passed'. His words have a triple meaning. First the obvious one of recalling Glyndŵr to mind, but secondly he hints at the idea that the Welsh prince is a sort of sleeping champion, a saviour in waiting. It is not really known when or where Glyndŵr actually died and this has given strength to the mythology that he is slumbering in some cavern somewhere waiting for the hour of need. Thirdly, Borrow is recalling his own 'times that are passed', the days when as a young man he first came across the poetry of Iolo Goch and made faltering attempts to translate it. The memory of those more innocent times, contrasted with the coarsening influence of the years is deeply moving to him and he covers his face and weeps.

Thirty-nine of Iolo Goch's poems have survived and of these three are about Glyndŵr. It is surprising to learn that he also addressed poems to the English king Edward III and Edward's great grandson Roger Mortimer, but he lived in troubled times. The fourteenth century was marred by the Black Death and social turmoil consequent upon it, and Iolo's first concern was the maintenance of social order. Indeed his *Llys Owain Glyndŵr* (Owain Glyndŵr's Court) eulogises the peaceful life of a Welsh gentleman prior to the rebellion of 1400. Borrow's translation may not stand up well in comparison to later efforts, but this need not be a problem for the non-specialist reader who approaches the poem as a depiction of Glyndŵr's domestic life, a document almost, rather than a work of literature.

Sycharth.

Borrow describes Owain Glyndŵr's hill at Sycharth as

> . . . the work of nature, save and except that to a certain extent it has been modified by the hand of man. It is somewhat conical and consists of two steps or gradations, where two fosses scooped out of the hill go round it, one above the other, the lower one embracing considerably the most space. Both these fosses are about six feet deep, and at one time doubtless were bricked, as stout large, red bricks are yet to be seen, here and there in their sides.

The mound is about eight metres high and twelve metres across at the top. Ditches surround it as Borrow describes and a large pool beneath it was no doubt the fish pond of Iolo Goch's poem. An excavation in the early nineteen sixties established the former presence of a timber-framed hall.

Owen Glendower's hill or mount at Sycharth . . . Tis water girdled wide about.

On his return to Llanrhaeadr-ym-Mochnant, Borrow made a detour via Llansilin so that he could visit the grave of the poet Huw Morys whose chair he had sat in some weeks before. He was very much in the territory of Sir Watkin here. A man who, as P.G. Wodehouse might have put it, held the rights to the high, the low and the middle justice over this part of Wales. The influence of Sir Watkin of Wynnstay is confirmed to this day by the name of the pub to which Borrow repaired for his customary jug of ale, The Wynnstay Inn. And there is no doubt as to Sir Watkin's hold over the low justice, for into the pub there burst a 'rabble rout of gamekeepers and river watchers', men in the employ of Sir Watkin who were in high spirits because they were celebrating the conviction in court that morning of two poachers. So high were their spirits in fact that one of them attempted to menace one of the locals, an old man who, however, stoutly defended himself with a stick, driving his assailant away and declaring him and his cronies to be 'a mixture of broken housekeepers, and fellows too stupid to learn a trade: a set of scamps fit for nothing in the world but to swear bodily against honest men.' This redoubtable if cantankerous old man had just been berating Borrow for his bad Welsh *and* bad English, both of which he took to be the language of South Wales.

'How do you know that I come from South Wales?' said I.

'By your English,' said the old fellow; 'anybody may know you are South Welsh by your English; it is so cursedly bad. But let's hear you speak a little Welsh; then I shall be certain as to who you are.'

I did as he bad me, saying a few words in Welsh.

'There's Welsh,' said the old fellow, 'but who but a South Welshman would talk Welsh in that manner? It's nearly as bad as your English.'

Borrow doesn't get the better of every exchange and nor does he mind telling a story against himself.

In the churchyard of Llansilin great gnarled old yew trees still stand as he describes. The ancient body of the church to which he refers dates from the second half of the fifteenth century, but it was restored in the late-nineteenth

The churchyard at Llansilin.

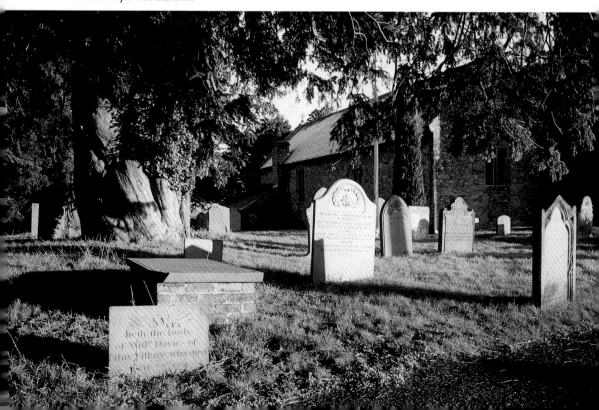

century and there is no sign now of 'the modern steeple which bears a gilded cock'. Of greatest interest to Borrow was a 'broad discoloured slab' beneath which lay 'the cold remains of the mighty Huw'. The inscription on the slab was already faded in Borrow's time – he could just make out '1709', the date of the poet's death. The stone can easily be found today, it having been surmounted by a more recent memorial.

On 28 October, Borrow set out for Bala intending first to visit the Pistyll Rhaeadr which is four miles from the town of Llanrhaeadr. On reaching the waterfall he was well rewarded for his efforts. Viewing it from a plank bridge, now replaced by one of steel, he writes:

> There are many remarkable cataracts in Britain and the neighbouring isles, even the little Celtic Isle of Man has its remarkable waterfall; but this Rhyadr, the grand cataract of North Wales, far exceeds them all in altitude and beauty, though it is inferior to several of them in the volume of its flood. I never saw water falling so gracefully, so much like thin beautiful threads as here.

The visitor of today will not be disappointed, although the falls are an even more popular destination for tourists and hikers than they were in Borrow's time, and to visit them in any degree of solitude it is advisable to go either early in the morning or very much out of season. Borrow goes on to describe the feature which for him slightly mars the beauty of the falls: 'An ugly black bridge or semi-circle of rock... which intercepts the sight, and prevents it from taking in the whole fall at once.' As he gazed, a woman came up to him and guided him to a higher viewpoint on the left-hand side of the fall almost on a level with this semi-circle of rock. On Borrow observing that this was a bridge more suited to spirits than people, she replied that nevertheless she had once seen a Russian man perform the heart-stopping feat of crossing it: 'He wriggled up the side like an eel, till he got to the top, when he stood upright for a minute, and then slid down on the other side.'

Before leaving the *pistyll*, Borrow took refreshments offered by the woman who had guided him and signed a visitors book. An earlier visitor had left a Welsh verse in the book which Borrow translated:

> Foaming and frothing from mountainous height,
> Roaring like thunder the Rhyadr falls;
> Though its silvery splendour the eye may delight,
> Its fury the heart of the bravest appals.

Even allowing that this is a translation, his verse never seems to achieve the strength of his prose. Compare, for example, his prose description of the waterfall:

What shall I liken it to? I scarcely know, unless to an immense skein of silk agitated and disturbed by tempestuous blasts, or to the long tail of a grey courser at furious speed. Through the profusion of long silvery threads or hairs, or what looked like such, I could here and there see the black sides of the crag down which the Rhyadr precipitated itself with something between a boom and a roar.

Borrow was now shown the way over the hills above the *pistyll* by the husband of the woman who had guided him to the falls. This man was a small farmer, a tenant of Sir Watkin's, who grazed his sheep on the moorlands. From time to time the farmer would catch grazing sheep and examine them to discover whether they were suffering from *pwd* or 'moor disorder'. Borrow, always happy to enter into conversation about farming matters, and never reluctant to display his knowledge was able to recommend a decoction of horehound as a remedy for the condition. Every now and again the farmer's dogs would surprise grouse or *ceiliog y grug*, birds which, the farmer said, 'are supposed to be very good eating, but . . . not food for the like of me. It goes to feed the rich Saxons in Caer Ludd', Caer Ludd being Ludlow.

There are few clues in the text as to the route they took over the moors, but those who wish to go across country rather than return to Llan Rhaeadr by road may decide to pick up the public path which circles Moel Mawn on the north east. Pursuing that to the south brings the walker out east of Llangynog on the minor road which joins the B4391 to Bala. Alternatively, by turning to the south-west at OS 073 290 it is possible to reach the Bala road at Pencraig.

Having reached the road Borrow headed north-west for Bala. Turning, he looked at the hills he had come across. 'There they stood, darkly blue, a rain cloud, like ink, hanging over their summits,' and he exclaims 'Oh, the wild hills of Wales, the land of old renown and wonder, the land of Arthur and Merlin.' Not even the rain could dismay him for he had his trusty umbrella which he proceeds to eulogise. He still had some miles to go over dreary, moory hills. When he says 'he crossed a bridge at the bottom of the valley and presently saw a road branching to the right' he was probably crossing Afon Caletwr, a tributary to the Dee. He had to stop to ask his way, but soon found himself approaching the familiar scenery of Llyn Tegid.

In Bala at the White Lion Inn once more, Borrow was cheered by the light and warmth of the coffee room which contrasted so happily with the 'gloomy, desolate places' through which he had come, but dismayed to find that the excellent Tom Jenkins was no longer working at the hotel now that the summer was over. Seasonal work and seasonal prosperity are hazards, then as now, in a country where tourism is one of the main industries.

In the absence of Tom Jenkins and even his beer, for this alas was quite literally at the bottom of the barrel, Borrow reacquainted himself with two

I never saw water falling so gracefully, so much like thin beautiful threads as here.

people in that inn at Bala. The one a real life acquaintance, in the shape of Dr Jones whom he had previously met in Cerrigydrudion, the other an apparition, but nevertheless real, the very embodiment of the Wolverhampton hog merchant of whom he had dreamed in Llangollen:

> He was an immense man, weighing I should say at least eighteen stone, with brown hair, thinnish whiskers, half-ruddy, half-tallowy complexion, and dressed in a brown sporting coat, drab breeches and yellow-topped boots . . . the exact image of the Wolverhampton gent . . . except that he did not appear to be more than seven- or eight-and-twenty, whereas the hog-merchant looked at least fifty.

In the morning Borrow sat down to another hearty breakfast:

> What a breakfast! pot of hare; ditto of trout; pot of prepared shrimps; tin of sardines; beautiful beef-steak; eggs, muffin; large loaf, and butter, not forgetting capital tea. There's a breakfast for you!

At dinner, which he took in the middle of the day, he was offered a 'noble goose' to which he did 'ample justice'. He ate and drank with relish and his feats at the table seem almost as impressive as his marathon walks.

The day being Sunday, Borrow attended two church services. In the morning he went to a church low down by the lake which he calls Llan uwch Llyn, but

The church at Llanycil.

which may have been Llanycil because he describes it as being in 'a little village close by, on the side of the lake'. He attended the service with the landlord of the inn who talked about how the Church of England had begun to make a comeback against Methodism chiefly by imitating the methods of its ministers. In the evening he attended the service in the old church in Bala. He was both pleased by the preaching of the vicar, a Mr Pugh, and charmed by the singing of the young women who 'seemed to have voices of wonderful power'. His chambermaid told him that these young women had once been Methodist girls but, having been converted had been the cause of a great many more conversions, because all the young men would follow them to church. 'That's a thing of course', Borrow concurs, 'If the Church gets the girls she is quite sure of the fellows.'

Borrow always seems pleased to report indications of a renewal in the fortunes of the Church of England, but he was really too optimistic on behalf of the Church. There was a great national Nonconformist Revival in 1859, only five years after Borrow's first Welsh tour and three years before the publication of *Wild Wales*. One might expect more sympathy from Borrow for the Nonconformists. He was sympathetic to the common people of Wales and, above all, an enthusiast for their language. Chapel life was entirely based on Welsh, by contrast the Church was a foreign English import.

CHAPTER NINE

Bala to Machynlleth

On Monday, Borrow set out on his journey once more. His conversation with the landlord is instructive because it reminds us how much more common the practice of walking long distances used to be. There is no doubt that even in his own times Borrow was a prodigious walker, but we should note that when he had consulted the landlord as to the best place to make his next stop, the landlord had recommended Mallwyd which was distant some thirty miles over difficult roads. As second best he had recommended Dinas Mawddwy, still a distance of twenty-eight miles. The point is that the landlord shows no surprise that such a long journey should be made by foot in one day. At any rate Borrow set out on one of the most impressive legs of an impressive journey. On a gloomy day he walked the entire south-eastern length of Llyn Tegid. On a fine day this is a delightful journey and one which can now be accomplished on the little tourist train. The lake contains in legend what its artificial neighbour, Llyn Celyn, contains in fact: a submerged town. The lad with whom Borrow falls into step explains:

> A fine city it was, full of fine houses, towers and castles, but with neither church nor chapel, for the people neither knew God nor cared for Him, and thought of nothing but singing and dancing and other wicked things.

And so the city was inundated and only a poor harpist was spared.

At Llanuwchllyn, Borrow turned south following the course of Afon Twrch. At Tŷ Nant, which is marked on the Ordnance Survey, he met a woman with no English. Her face looked the picture of kindness. He felt that he was now 'indeed in Wales amongst the real Welsh'. He toiled on upwards and reaching the top of the pass he paused to look back. Beneath him was the valley, far away a glimpse of Llyn Tegid and to the north-west the Arrans. This is one of the highest passes in Wales that can be negotiated by motor car, though even today the road is single track and becomes quite impassable in snow in all but the most robust of four-wheel-drive vehicles.

Making the steep descent down the other side of the pass, Borrow reached a 'gloomy vale' at Pennant. There was a farmhouse in this vale, as there still is, from which there emerged two men, father and son. Borrow enters into conversation with them learning that the waterfall which he could see at the end

Looking down into the valley Cwm Cynllwyd.

of the valley carries the waters of the Dyfi. Hearing that the Dyfi is thought to rise from a deep lake at the foot of Aran Fawr, he asks about crocodiles and 'efync'. The farmer thinks they have all been killed long ago by Hu Gadarn. The three men were standing beneath a craggy mount called the Tap Nyth yr Eryri or 'the top nest of the eagles' as Borrow translates it. The older man told him that there had been no eagles there for a generation. Changing the subject, Borrow now asks about the red-haired robbers of Mawddwy. At first the farmer responds coldly, but then finding that his questioner knows something about the subject, he softens and replies that the robbers had long ago been hanged. We will meet the red-haired robbers again a little later, but for the moment we will observe that these passages reveal something of Borrow's technique. At first sight he is merely ranging inquisitively over a variety of topics, firing off questions almost at random, but in fact he has brought his subjects together and united them, for they have the common theme of extinction.

Hurrying on, Borrow next met a carpenter, a great admirer of the works of Huw Morys whose poetry had given him a love for the sights of nature. Borrow

Rocky outcrops at Craig yr Ogof.

found him to be a very sensible man. Perhaps he was influenced not only by their common enthusiasm for Huw Morys, but also by the carpenter's Church-of-England sympathies. He passed on through Llanymawddwy, learning the name of the mountain which rises behind it, Pen Foel-y-ffridd which he translates as 'the party-coloured moel'. *'Ffridd'* in fact means sheep walk or mountain pasture, but perhaps Borrow is referring to Foel yr hydd which means the stag mountain. 'Scenery of the wildest and most picturesque description was rife . . . what a valley!' he exclaims. Yet the next valley was even 'wilder and stranger' if possible. He was excited to learn the name of the village Aber-Cywarch, for this was where Ellis Wynne had composed his *Sleeping Bard* which Borrow had translated in his youth. *Visions of the Sleeping Bard* was the first of his Welsh translations to be published. Although it was written much

Tap Nyth-yr-Eryr.

earlier, it did not appear until 1860 and then only when Borrow put up the money for its publication. Even so, it sold quite well and its success may have persuaded Borrow and John Murray to go ahead with the publication of *Wild Wales* in 1862.

The river Dyfi at an infant stage.

Night was coming on as he reached Dinas Mawddwy. It seemed to him little more than 'a collection of filthy huts', 'a dirty squalid place', and not improved by the 'sounds of drunken revelry' and 'fierce-looking red-haired men' staggering about. Borrow went on to Mallwyd where he put up at the hotel which is now called the Brigands Inn. The fierce-looking red-haired men had put Borrow in mind of the Red-haired Bandits of Mawddwy. The bandits had established themselves in these parts in the fifteenth century. Thomas Pennant has this to say of them:

> After the wars of the houses of York and Lancaster, multitudes of felons and outlaws established in these parts, stealing and driving whole herds of cattle from one county to another. The traditions respecting these banditti are still extremely strong. I was told that they were so feared that travellers did not dare to go the common road to Shrewsbury but passed over the summits of the mountains to avoid their haunts. The inhabitants placed scythes in the chimneys of their houses to prevent the felons coming down to surprise them in the night, some of which are still to be seen to this day.

Pennant was writing in the 1770s. The bandits had disappeared long before and the fierce red-haired men whom Borrow had seen were in fact drunken miners, a fractious and Godless lot according to the maid at the hotel. The name of the hotel too recalls the bandits, although in Borrow's day it was known as the Peniarth after the Peniarth estate, to which it belonged.

The Brigands Inn at Mallwyd, formerly known as the Peniarth Inn.

The church at Mallwyd.

The following day Borrow intended to go no further than Machynlleth, for him a trivial twelve miles, so he spent some time looking round Mallwyd. He describes it thus:

> Mallwyd is a small but pretty village. The church is a long edifice standing on a slight elevation on the left of the road. Its pulpit is illustrious from having for many years been occupied by one of the very celebrated men of Wales, namely Doctor John Davies, author of the great Welsh and Latin dictionary, an imperishable work. An immense yew tree grows in the churchyard and partly overshadows the road with its branches. The parsonage stands about a hundred yards to the south of the church near a grove of firs.

Today, the motorist might be forgiven for thinking Mallwyd little more than a roundabout with a rather interesting old pub on the corner. But for those who stop there and for those who choose more leisurely means of travel, it repays inspection. The original church was founded in AD 525 and much of the present stone building predates the year 1641 which is carved on the great oak beam at the porch entrance. Surmounting the beam is a curious bone, said to be the rib and vertebra of a prehistoric ox. The unusual planked tower was erected in

1651 and would already have been two hundred years old when Borrow saw it. Dr John Davies came to Mallwyd as rector in 1604. He produced not only the Welsh-Latin dictionary that Borrow mentions, but also a Welsh grammar in Latin and he is considered largely responsible for the revised version of William Morgan's Bible which appeared in 1620, as well as the prayer book which was published in the following year.

Taking a lingering look back at the mountainous district he was leaving, Borrow headed south along the A470. First in the company of two boys and then alone, he passed through the village of Cwmlline and soon reached Cemais, where a remarkable little adventure occurred. He stopped at an inn for some ale and gave his order in Welsh to the boy who was waiting. The boy then shouted a warning 'Cumro' to the rest of the customers, as if to alert them that this newcomer could understand Welsh. Upon this the assembled company fell silent and stared suspiciously at Borrow. Borrow sat down and waited for his ale. Ale was brought. The silence deepened. Suspicion was maintained; but Borrow had nerve. He 'determined to comport himself in a manner which should to a certain extent afford them ground for suspicion', so he drew out his notebook and pencil and jotted down a description of the scene. He gives us a picture of 'the comfortable kitchen', the 'immense grate and brilliant fire', 'seven fine large men'. They are dressed mostly in brown coats, broad-brimmed hats and yellowish corduroy breeches with gaiters. There are two dogs, 'a fine brindled greyhound' lying on the slate floor by the fire and a shepherd's dog which wanders about and scratches at the door as if trying to get out . . . Borrow continues, as did the silence. Eventually he finished up his ale and left, but after walking fifty yards down the street he turned round to see the whole company staring at him from the door of the pub. Taking out his notebook once more and resuming his jottings, he sent them all panicking back into the inn.

In Machynlleth, as was his habit, Borrow put up at the principal hotel, another Wynnstay Arms though not the one which now stands in Maengwyn Street. In Borrow's time this was the Commercial Hotel. The original Wynnstay was behind and to the right of the clock tower in buildings now occupied by a

The old market hall, demolished in the 1870s, where Borrow would have attended the hearing against the salmon poacher.

newsagent and a building society. The old coaching yard can still be seen if you pass through the archway almost behind the clock tower, although the stables have given way to modern garages, and it must have been here that Borrow held his conversations with the hotel ostler.

In the morning Borrow breakfasted with a lawyer whose brief that day was to defend a man charged with salmon poaching. The fishing rights which had allegedly been violated belonged to Sir Watkin, whose bumptious gamekeepers we have met causing such a rowdy scene in the pub at Llansilin. Borrow determined to attend the hearing and found his way to the market hall above which the court was housed. The chairman of the magistrates, mysteriously referred to by Borrow as 'Lord V-' was in fact Lord Vane. His family owned Plas Machynlleth, which now houses the 'Celtica' exhibition, until the nineteen forties. The case against the accused consisted of the evidence of two gamekeepers; the prosecution could not produce a body for, on finding that he was observed, the would-be poacher had flung the salmon back into deep water. However, despite the efforts of the defence to discredit the witnesses, the accused man was found guilty and ordered to pay four pounds. Not surprising, perhaps, because his reputation for illegal fishing was well known.

Machynlleth's distinctive clock tower now occupies the site of the old market hall.

Machynlleth is inescapably the town of Owain Glyndŵr, for it was here that he held his parliament in 1404, two years later than Borrow puts it. It was here too that he was crowned Prince of Wales in front of envoys from France, Scotland and Castile. He was then at the height of his fortunes having captured castles from Conway to Cardiff and three times having defeated or evaded punitive expeditions by the English king Henry Bolingbroke:

> Three times hath Henry Bolingbroke made head
> Against my power; thrice from the banks of Wye
> And sandy-bottom'd Severn have I sent him
> Bootless home and weather-beaten back.
> (Shakespeare, *King Henry IV Part One*, Act III scene I)

The parliament building, which is in Maengwyn Street, was restored to its present state in 1910-12. It now houses an exhibition which depicts Glyndŵr's place in Welsh history.

Borrow also mentions Dafydd Gam, the implacable enemy of Glyndŵr, who went to Machynlleth with the intention of assassinating him. Gam's plot was foiled and it is said that he was imprisoned in the Royal House, a medieval building which still survives, though it is very dilapidated, in Penrallt Street, just a short walk from Borrow's hotel.

The old Wynnstay Arms.

Two present day views of the Parliament House at Machynlleth.

Owain Glyndŵr's statue, sculpted by Alfred Turner RBS, stands on the imposing stairway of Cardiff City Hall. Born around 1354, there was nothing in Glyndŵr's early life to indicate the extraordinary heights to which he would rise. As a young man he studied law at the Inns of Court in London and even served the English Crown in a military capacity, taking part in the invasion of Scotland in 1385.

His uprising began in 1400 as the result of a territorial dispute with Reginald de Grey, made more bitter, complicated and political by recent events in England, where in 1399 Henry IV (Henry Bolinbroke) had seized the crown from Richard II. It was social and economic discontent and an underlying Welsh patriotism, together with Glyndŵr's princely lineage which turned the uprising into a national revolt. To this we must add Glyndŵr's military genius and his political and personal talents which made the revolt successful, at least for a while.

After 1405, Glyndŵr's fortunes began to decline. The Tripartite Indenture of that year, a plan made to divide England between himself, the Percys and the Mortimers, came to nothing. His alliance with France collapsed in 1407 and defeats in subsequent years led to the loss of Aberystwyth and Harlech castles. By 1413 the rebellion had definitely been suppressed. Glyndŵr himself was never betrayed or captured, and although it is thought he died in about 1416, the circumstances of his death are entirely shadowy, which has contributed greatly to his mythical importance.

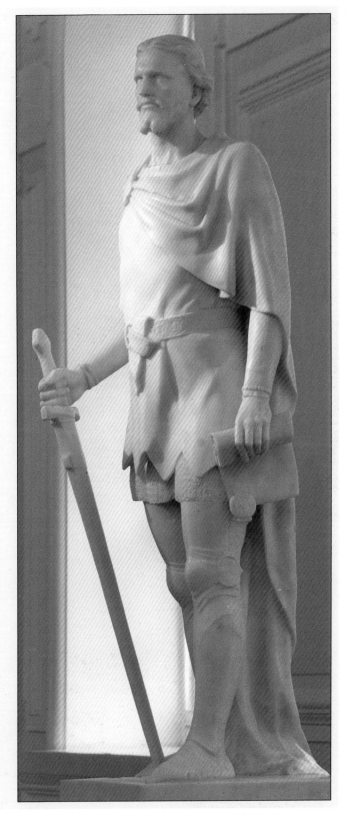

CHAPTER TEN

Machynlleth to Hafod

Borrow's next objective was Devil's Bridge or Pontarfynach and he sought advice as to the route from the hotel ostler. Despite the latter's warnings that the shorter way over the hills was an 'awful road' and indeed 'for the greater part . . . no road at all', Borrow determined to take it. All was well for the first few miles, for the track was good as far as Glaspwll, but from there on it

Ruined buildings of the Welsh Potsoi Mining Company.

deteriorated until his 'course lay over very broken ground where there was no path, at least that I could perceive'. He stopped to inquire directions, probably at Cefn Coch farm, and although he received them, they were only grudgingly given by two 'Saxon-hating Welsh women'.

The old ostler had warned that Borrow might meet the *Gŵr Drwg* or devil himself. Happily he encountered no such misfortune, but he did come upon a dangerous-looking vagabond, a man with a carbuncled face, narrow forehead and small malignant eyes, who did his best to direct him to the wrong path. This

Nant y Moch Reservoir.

was at 'Waen y Bwlch' as Borrow renders it which was probably *Gweunbwll* (OS 737 939). All in all, he was quite fortunate to stumble upon the workings of the Potosi Mining Company. These were actually at Esgair Hir which means Long Ridge, not Esgyrn Hirion or Long Bones as Borrow has it. On the ground today there remains a row of ruined buildings and in the corner of the most northerly of them there is a brick fireplace. Perhaps this is the very spot where Borrow talked with the young mining manager.

From Esgair Hir down to Ponterwyd, Borrow had a much easier time of it, for the mining company furnished him with a guide, thinking that he would get quite lost if he ventured further by himself. The terrain in these parts has changed beyond all recognition since the mid-nineteenth century, for the Nant y Moch valley is now filled by a great reservoir. There are a few clues in the text as to the route Borrow and his guide took and it is thought they descended to Ponterwyd by way of Dolrhuddlan and Bwlchystyllen.

On the way to Ponterwyd, Borrow questions his guide on the life of a miner and learns that his companion enjoys working underground, or would do so, if it were not for the 'noises made by the spirits of the hill in the mine. Sometimes they make such noises as frighten the poor fellow who works underground out of his senses.' It was a commonly held belief amongst miners that 'knockers' in the hill would guide them to the sources of the ore. At about this time a visitor to a mine near Llanidloes wrote that

> In a stranger there is awakened, when in a mine far within the bowels of the earth, a class of sensations wholly new to him. He hears the loud rushing of water which comes he knows not whence, the blows of hammers and picks, the falling of heavy fragments of rock, sometimes occasioning the vibration of the floor on which he stands, yet he sees none of the agents which produce these sounds

Perhaps the noises that Borrow's guide so complained of were the sounds of neighbouring workings being transmitted underground.

Safely arrived at the inn at Ponterwyd, Borrow paid off his guide and saw to his material needs in the shape of bread and cheese and ale. The landlord of the Gogerddan Arms, as the George Borrow Hotel was then called, was a rather supercilious individual whom Borrow lampoons as a 'remarkable personage in

whom were united landlord, farmer, poet, and mighty fine gentleman'. We know from the census records that this man's name was Thomas Holmes.

Many of the pubs and hotels where Borrow stayed are still standing, and in many cases their present incumbents are aware of his travels some hundred and fifty years ago, but only at Ponterwyd does the hotel actually bear his name. It was first named the 'George Borrow Hotel' in the 1920s.

He was thirty-four at Borrow's time and married to Elizabeth with whom he had six children. Relations between Borrow and Holmes started badly and went down hill thereafter. Borrow teases the landlord and his claims to a perfect knowledge of the Welsh language. He ends up by alarming Holmes into thinking that he has come to the area to rent a sheep farm. Intrusion by wealthy outsiders was resented in these parts because it forced up rents beyond the pockets of the local farmers. However, it is notable that, when he realises he has aroused the landlord's fears, Borrow backs off and becomes very soothing with:

The bridge at Ponterwyd in the 1860s and today.

'Come!' said I, 'don't be afraid; I wouldn't have all the farms in your country . . . If I talked about a farm it was because I am in the habit of talking about everything, being versed in all matters, do you see, *or affecting to be so* . . . [my italics]'

His words are effective at soothing the landlord, but they are also reassuring to the reader. By adding the self-deprecating 'affecting to be so' he laughs at himself, he admits that he can become a bit pompous at times and in so doing refreshes the reader who has become a little weary of his constant harangues.

The following morning Borrow set out for the Devil's Bridge in the company of a mining captain whom he had met in the pub at Ponterwyd, John Greaves from the county of Durham. Borrow regales his companion with boyhood memories of Durham County, while the latter reciprocates with an account of his life. Mining, particularly lead mining, was the principal industry in these parts in the middle of the nineteenth century and it attracted many immigrants from other parts of Britain, especially Cornwall and Devon. A search of the census records shows that there was a man from Durham County in Borrow's time. He was a William *Grieves*, not Greaves as Borrow has him. He worked in the mining industry as an ore dresser and he did have a son called John, but his family was much larger than the one Borrow describes. The historical Grieves had eight children, two of whom were miners.

While walking with John Greaves, Borrow is surprised to hear his companion claim friendship with the Duke of Newcastle, a former owner of the nearby Hafod estate. The reader too may be surprised. The north country link between Greaves and the Duke is spurious for the Duke of Newcastle had his seat at Clumber in Nottinghamshire and was in fact the Duke of Newcastle-under-Lyme, not the great northern city Newcastle-upon-Tyne. But the surprise goes deeper than this. Students of nineteenth-century history will find it very difficult to square Greaves's (or Borrow's) account of the Duke's character with what they know of his political career. The Duke of Newcastle was a strong opponent of reform, so much so that he attracted the attentions of the mob in London. In Nottinghamshire too he was on the receiving end of violent working-class action. When news of the House of Lords' rejection of the Reform Bill in 1831 reached Nottingham, outraged rioters ransacked and set fire to Nottingham Castle, owned but not inhabited by the Duke. His great house at Clumber was also laid to siege. It was not only the workers whose anger he aroused. His peers too were shocked – and they were not noted for their popular sympathies – when high-handedly he defended his summary eviction of tenants by asserting his absolute right to do as he would with his own. In short, if ever there was a die-hard Tory, Henry Pelham, Fourth Duke of Newcastle, was he.

He has been described as 'arguably the most unpopular individual in England' and it has been suggested that he sought out Hafod as a refuge, where safe from the attentions of an angry mob he could live quietly amidst a quiescent peasantry. Why then does the Duke get such a good press in *Wild Wales*? Greaves reports how 'his Grace was wonderfully fond of farming and improving – and a wonderful deal of good he did, reclaiming thousands of acres of land which was before good for nothing, and building capital farm-houses and offices for his tenants'. Borrow too reiterates Greaves's favourable report of the Duke, in Chapter 89 describing him as 'a kind and philanthropic nobleman and a great friend of agriculture'.

It might have been the Duke's anti-Catholicism that appealed to Borrow, for the former was a vigorous opponent of Catholic Emancipation as well as parliamentary reform, but there is no certain proof that it was. In fact, whether the Duke's despotic past has been exaggerated or not, there is little or no evidence of untrammelled autocracy on his mid-Wales estates. He attended to the material fabric of Hafod, rebuilding the house and repairing the church at Eglwys Newydd, but he also attended to humbler dwellings rebuilding cottages both on the estate and at the nearby village of Cwmystwyth. He established a school for the villagers' children as well as those of his own servants and he showed some leniency towards rent arrears when times were hard.

The Duke of Newcastle also greatly aggrandised the inn where Borrow stayed

The Hafod Arms at Devil's Bridge, built by the Duke of Newcastle.

at Devil's Bridge. Described by Borrow as an immense lofty cottage, the Hafod Arms still stands with its impressive projecting eaves. Its most splendid rooms are named the 'Duke of Newcastle Suite' after its builder. It was from here that Borrow set out to explore the 'profound hollow with all the appearance of an extinct volcano' into which pour the waters of the Rheidol and the Mynach. His description suggests that he descended from the southern side and re-ascended by the same route and he captures the excitement and even the fear of the experience:

> The fall, which is split into two, is thundering beside you; foam, foam, foam is flying all about you; the basin or cauldron is boiling frightfully below you; hirsute rocks are frowning terribly above you, and above them forest trees, dank and wet with spray and mist, are distilling drops in showers from their boughs.

To view the Devil's Bridge itself, he descended a 'precipitous dingle' on the eastern side of the road to 'a small platform in a crag'.

> Below you now is a frightful cavity, at the bottom of which the waters of the Monk's River which comes tumbling from a glen to the east, whirl, boil and hiss in a horrid pot or cauldron, called in the language of the country Twll yn y graig, or the hole in the rock, in a manner truly tremendous. On your right is a slit, probably caused by volcanic force, through which the waters after whirling in the cauldron eventually escape . . . nearly above you, crossing the slit, which is partially wrapt in darkness,

is the far-famed bridge, the Bridge of the Evil Man, a work which though crumbling and darkly grey does much honour to the hand which built it, whether it was the hand of Satin or of a monkish architect, for the arch is chaste and beautiful, far superior in every respect, except in safety and utility, to the one above it.

The falls and the bridge are very much commercialised these days. There is nothing new about this. As far back as the late eighteenth century, Thomas Johnes was trying to encourage tourism to the area though the number of visitors was much smaller in his day. Really to appreciate the full impact of a visit in days gone by, we need to think ourselves back to a time before television and motion pictures.

Nineteenth-century engraving of the Devil's Bridge. Borrow would have crossed the eighteenth-century structure which surmounts it.

The Falls of the Mynach glimpsed through the dense vegetation of today. A tiny sapling oak (left) has rooted on the moss-laden branch of its parent.

Borrow does not mention the legend associated with the Devil's Bridge: the old woman who had lost her cow on the other side of the gorge, the Devil who appeared in disguise promising to build a bridge if he could have the soul of the first living creature to cross it and the trickery of the old woman who enticed her dog to make the first crossing. Today's sightseers will find themselves unable to avoid it, but if they tire of it they may be pleased with the words of the antiquarian Meyrick who in 1810 wrote:

The three bridges as they now appear

> In a tour through North Wales, written in 1803, at Birmingham, a traveller has coined a tradition of an old woman and her cow, and attributed it to the Welsh peasantry. Be it said, for the honour of the Welsh peasantry, that they are ignorant of such a ridiculous story, and that it can only be traced to an author, the whole of whose composition proves his ignorance of the manners, or language, of a people he attempts to deride.

In reality the bridge was built by the monks of Strata Florida.

We do hear from Borrow the story of the 'Plant de Bat', three robbers who lived in a cave at the foot of the falls of the Mynach. Reputedly they were the children of Mathew Evans – hence they should be called *Plant Mat*, or Mathew's children – who kept a pub in Tregaron around the middle of the fifteenth century. For many years they plied their trade with impunity, but eventually, overreaching themselves and committing murder, they were captured and executed.

During his stay at the Hafod Arms, Borrow twice retraced his steps. First to visit the bridge over the Rheidol, the so-called Parson's Bridge. He found the scenery there rather less spectacular than around the Devil's Bridge:

> The river was rushing and surging, the pot was boiling and roaring, and everything looked wild and savage; but the locality for awfulness and

mysterious gloom could not compare with that on the east side of the Devil's Bridge, nor for sublimity and grandeur with that on the west.

His second and longer expedition was made to Pumlumon. He made his ascent from the inn at Castell Dyffryn where he hired a shepherd as a guide. Reaching the summit of the mountain he stood upon the cairn and surveyed the scene.

A mountainous wilderness extended on every side, a waste of russet-coloured hills, with here and there a black craggy summit. No signs of life or cultivation were to be discovered, and the eye might search in vain for a grove or even a single tree.

A mountainous wilderness extended on every side, a waste of russet-coloured hills.

Turning to his guide Borrow observes 'This does not seem to be a country of much society', and the guide agrees with him: 'Pumlummon is not a sociable country, sir; nothing to be found in it, but here and there a few sheep or a shepherd'. The sheep and the sheep farming persist. The mines which were active in Borrow's day now all lie in ruins, but new industries have arrived, for example, forestry. Today the searching eye alights much more easily on the plantations of the Forestry Commission. Energy too is a new industry. In his wildest imagination Borrow could hardly have foreseen the arrival of the great man-made lake of Nant y Moch, or the enormous dam at its southern extremity which was built in the 1960s to supply Aberystwyth with hydroelectric power. More recently, and controversially, wind-power has been introduced, but despite such changes little has occurred really to disrupt the vast emptiness. Less poetically than Borrow, but perhaps not less aptly, these great stretches of wilderness have been described by hikers as a sodden weariness.

Part of Borrow's purpose in being on the mountain was to visit the sources of the three great rivers, the Rheidol, the Severn and the Wye. First his guide escorted him to the source of the Rheidol, the small lake Llyn Llygad Rheidol or the 'lake of the eye of the Rheidol'. However, whether knowingly or not, it seems that his guide misled him as to the true source of the Severn, taking him instead to the pools which feed Afon Tarennig. It has been suggested that guides, more wary than their hirers of the need to get down from the mountain in daylight, often humoured them by taking them to this dummy source. The real source of the Severn lies a good two and a half miles north east of that of the Rheidol. From his description it is probable that Borrow was shown the real

origin of the Wye, but his assessment that 'all three [sources] are contained within the compass of a mile' cannot be squared with his having been shown the genuine origin of all three.

When he left Devil's Bridge, Borrow headed south-east along the B4574. At what was then the entrance to the Hafod estate, he passed under a rough stone archway which still bestrides the road. This was erected in 1810 by Thomas Johnes to mark the jubilee of George III. Thomas

The infant Wye as it bubbles off the slopes of Pumlumon.

The great dam at Nant y Moch.

I saw a park before me, through which the road led after passing under a stately gateway.

Johnes had first come to these parts in 1780, having inherited the Hafod estates on the death of his father. He had seen in these then barren hills a potential Eden and, fired with enthusiasm for ideas of the Picturesque, he had set about the development of the house and grounds. In his time he had been enthusiastic agricultural improver, forester, collector, connoisseur and scholar. Nash had been involved in the building of his house. It was painted by Turner and John 'Warwick' Smith and many others and the grounds were famously described by George Cumberland in his *An Attempt to Describe Hafod* (1796). He was also a very considerate landlord, such that the *Gentleman's Magazine* was able to speak in his obituary of his benevolence 'which stooped to comfort the fireside of the lowliest cottager'. In fact, one wonders whether Borrow hasn't confused the Duke of Newcastle with Thomas Johnes when he

Hafod House in c. 1850. *A truly fairy place it looked, beautiful but fantastic, in the building of which three styles of architecture seemed to have been employed. At the southern end was a Gothic tower; at the northern was an Indian pagoda; the middle part had much the appearance of a Grecian villa. The walls were of resplendent whiteness, and the windows which were numerous shone with beautiful gilding.*

describes the former as a 'kind and philanthropic nobleman and a great friend of agriculture'.

The Johnes family suffered terrible misfortunes at Hafod. First, the house burnt down in 1807. Then, in 1811, their only daughter died. This was Mariamne rather than Mary as Borrow calls her, whose monument he went to see in the church at Eglwys Newydd. Sculpted by Chantrey, whose secretary was a friend of Borrow, the monument itself was to suffer misfortune when in 1932 the church was burnt down. Johnes died in 1816 and so disordered were his financial affairs that the estate ended up in Chancery until the Duke of Newcastle bought it in 1832. He sold it to Henry Hoghton in 1845 who

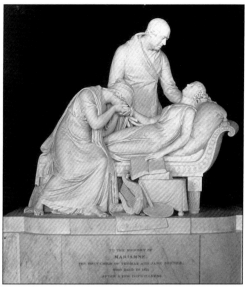

Francis Chantrey's memorial to Mariamne Jones.

was still in ownership when Borrow saw it in 1854. By that time considerable adaptations had been made.

Looking across Hafod lands from the east.

Engraving of Nash's library. For Borrow the real tragedy of the fire at Hafod was the loss of the manuscripts of Edward Lhuyd which were contained in the library's Sebright Collection. Described by Borrow as 'the best Celtic scholar of his time', Lhuyd published the first, and only, volume of his *Archaeologia Britannica* in 1707. It was a foundation for the modern study of Celtic languages, and a strong influence on Borrow who as a young man made pencilled notes in Lhuyd's work in the Norwich Public Library. Borrow's journeys in some ways echo those of Lhuyd who travelled extensively in the Celtic countries and was even once imprisoned in Brittany, as Borrow was in Spain.

CHAPTER ELEVEN

Hafod to Llandovery

Leaving Hafod and turning south, Borrow crossed the Ystwyth at Pontrhydygroes or the Bridge of the Ford of the Cross. We are still on the pilgrims' route to Strata Florida. Hardly had he done so than he found himself in the midst of a wedding party consisting of young men wearing crimson favours and young women in blue tunics and sharp crowned hats. Far from answering his questions courteously, these smartly dressed young people set upon him, jeering at his Welsh, hooting even more loudly at his English and goading him to return to north Wales where such a rustic and a bumpkin would not be so out of place:

'Go back, David, to your goats in Anglesey, you are not wanted here.'

Some people say that because he had learnt his Welsh, his colloquial Welsh, in the North, he was readily mistaken for a north Welshman by people in south Wales. This won't really do for an argument because we have seen how in north Wales he was sometimes mistaken for a south Welshman. Indeed, he had also been mistaken for a Breton and a Spaniard! His Welsh, we may assume, therefore, was outlandish wherever he spoke it. We cannot be sure if this incident is fabricated or not, for the notes in his diary are very brief at this point, consisting of:

Bridge the bridal company young men with crimson favours – Women in ancient Welsh dresses blue tunics – pointed hats – the bridge Pont y Groes . . .

The lack of material here is not sufficient in itself for us to be able to say that he invented the scene, that it is another example of the 'stirring incidents' that his publisher requested should be inserted into Wild Wales, for we know that Borrow's memory was prodigious and he needed very few notes to reconstruct his story. My own view is that he presents this scene, real or partly fabricated, with himself as the butt to emphasise that he is passing into south Wales.

He walked on, climbing the hill, not descending as he mistakenly writes. On the right were 'immense works . . . in full play and activity', with 'engines clanging and puffs of smoke ascending from tall chimneys'; the great mining works of Level Fawr. At Ysbyty Ystwyth, where there was formerly a hospice for pilgrims, he found only a few cottages and a shabby-looking church. Now there is a second small church, by no means shabby, and, until recently a great chapel which rose in defiant superiority, a monumental reminder of the triumph of chapel over church, and a reminder too of how Borrow misjudged the importance of Nonconformity in Wales.

A little further on, just passed the Afon Marchnant, he stopped into a wayside inn for ale. He is rather unkind to the widow who runs the house, ticking her off because she has substituted wormwood or bitter root in her beer for the more expensive hops. There were several alehouses in this area at Borrow's time, hostelries in which the miners would drown their sorrows and spend their hard-earned pay. Now only one remains, but that appropriately is called the Miners Arms.

The landscape was very dreary in this region. A bleak moor brought Borrow to Ffair-rhos which he describes as 'a miserable village, consisting of a few half-ruined cottages'. From there he looked south into the valley which contains Strata Florida Abbey. 'The whole scene was cheerless. Sullen hills were all around'. He was close to the abbey now, but first he had to pass through Pontrhydfendigaid, and here we have another scene where he emphasises himself as a stranger. The men glared sullenly at him and let their tobacco smoke curl into his face. The women fell silent and leered contemptuously at him. Even the animals were hostile. Immense swine lying in the street turned up their snouts at him as he passed. It is the very image of a traveller unwelcome in a foreign land. Everything is indifferent or hostile, the people, the animals, even the landscape.

However, the people were helpful enough when he asked directions to the abbey and he turned right after the bridge to walk the two remaining miles. To the north of the church which stands beside the abbey ruins, he found the yew tree beneath which the mortal remains of Dafydd ap Gwilym are said to lie. There he knelt down and, kissing the root of the tree, recited lines of Gruffudd Gryg addressed to the tree:

> Beneath thee lies, by cold Death bound,
> The tongue for sweetness once renown'd.

The local tenant farmer then came up and the two of them fell into conversation about the abbey ruins:

Borrow: It was a wonderful place once; you merely see the ruins of it now. It was pulled down at the Reformation.

Farmer: Why was it pulled down then?

Borrow: Because it was a house of idolatry to which people used to resort by hundreds to worship images. Had you lived at that

Central doorway in the ruined west front of Strata Florida Abbey.

time you would have seen people down on their knees before stocks and stones, worshipping them, kissing them and repeating penillion to them.

Farmer: What fools! How thankful I am that I live in wiser days.

There can be no unconscious irony here. Borrow is surely laughing at himself. People kneeling on the ground, kissing the roots of trees, repeating poetry, these are the very things he has just been doing himself. Having spent the whole of Chapter 86 writing about ap Gwilym, having praised 'the genius of this wonderful man', having left the reader in no doubt about the importance of his pilgrimage, Borrow proceeds to make fun of himself and his obsessions and even his anti-papist prejudices. This is certainly one of the most unexpected, curious and enjoyable episodes in the book.

Night was approaching now, and Borrow had to hurry along to reach Tregaron. He headed south along what is now the B4343. The bridge which a passing carter named as Pont 'Vleer' must be Pont Fflur which crosses a river of the same name. He noticed the glimmer of the lake at Maeslyn and mentions two or three houses on the left. Today there are the ruins of two buildings amidst the trees opposite the lake as he describes. The lake is on the edge of Cors Caron, or Tregaron Bog, a wetland which supports important plant and animal life. It has been described by William Condry as 'a landscape of the past miraculously surviving into modern Wales'.

Dafydd ap Gwilym flourished for much of the fourteenth century and is described in *The New Companion to the Literature of Wales* as 'The most distinguished of medieval Welsh poets and perhaps the greatest Welsh poet of all time.' Borrow admires him too as 'The greatest of his country's songsters, well calculated by nature to do honour to the most polished age and the most widely-spoken language.' It is unlikely, however, that Borrow's admiration began in quite such early youth as he would have us believe in *Lavengro*. His first Welsh enthusiasms were for the poetry of Goronwy Owen and Iolo Goch and he only began to attempt translations of ap Gwilym's work in the 1840s. It has to be admitted that his attempts don't read very well today. Compare, for example, his rendering of '*Y Niwl*' ('The Mist') in chapter 17 to the translation by Rachel Bromwich in *Dafydd ap Gwilym, Poems* in the Welsh Classics series.

However, we must be fair to Borrow. The translator of today begins with much more reliable materials. Borrow unwittingly translated two poems, ostensibly by ap Gwilym, which were actually forgeries written by Iolo Morganwg and which were not unmasked until the 1920s. Then again, Borrow was more ambitious than the modern translator. He attempts a poetic rendering in place of the original whereas his modern counterpart offers an English translation often only to serve as an aid to understanding something of the original. In the final analysis, the quality of Borrow's translations is probably not the most important consideration because he is enjoyed for his enthusiastic approach rather than the literary merit of his work.

From this point down to Tregaron he walked in the company of a retired drover who regaled him with stories of Twm Siôn Cati, a Robin Hood-like figure of the sixteenth century. Twm's real name was Thomas Jones and he was the illegitimate son of Sion ap Dafydd and Catherine. Borrow is not alone in ascribing his parentage to Sir John Wynn of Gwydir. The antiquarian Meyrick writing more than forty years before Borrow has this to say about him:

On a hill, south-east of [Tregaron], are shewn the ruins of Fountaingate, called by the people, Plas Twm Sion Catty, where the natural son of Sir

John Wynne, of Gwydyr, known by the name of 'Twm o'Sion a Catty', that is, 'Tom, the son of John and Catherine', lived. His real name was Thomas Jones, and he flourished from about A.D. 1590, to 1630. He was also esteemed as an eminent antiquary and poet; but he is better known from the tricks attributed to him as a robber, many of which are still retained in the memory of the people in Cardiganshire and Caermarthenshire.

In 1828 a popular account of Twm's exploits appeared called *The Adventures and Vagaries of Twm Shon Catti* by T.J. Llewelyn Prichard.

Borrow's account of his conversation with the drover is a little puzzling. When he asks the drover 'Have you given up the business of drover long?', the drover replies 'Oh yes; given him up a long time, ever since domm'd railroad came into fashion.' The railway did not reach Tregaron until 1866, four years after the publication of *Wild Wales*, when it did in fact

Statue of a drover at Llandovery.

destroy the droving industry. Did the drover mean that the beasts were driven to south Wales or to the border and then taken on by train? Or did Borrow have the conversation with the drover elsewhere, where the railway had already arrived, and insert it here? In any event the presence of a drover is appropriate because Tregaron was one of the great centres of the livestock industry in the first half of the nineteenth century. In *The Drovers' Roads of Wales*, Shirley Toulson tells us that some of the big dealers in the area would employ as many as twenty drovers. Cattle would be gathered in a field behind the Talbot Arms, the hotel where Borrow stayed. From there they would be driven to Pumsaint where herds from the west would meet them, and so on to Lampeter and Llandovery.

The drover's assertion that Tregaron is 'not quite so big as London, but very good place' would not have been quite as laughable then as it sounds now because the activity generated by droving together with the town's native cloth industry would have made it a

The Talbot Hotel at Tregaron.

very busy place indeed. The Talbot Arms, where Borrow 'experienced very good entertainment', still stands in the square and offers a 'drover's lunch', a locally appropriate alternative to the ubiquitous 'ploughman's'. He did not stay there long but set out for Llanddewibrefi after briefly visiting the church. He was still following the road which is now the B4343 and he mentions passing through Abercoed and Abercarfan as well as Nantydderwen which he renders as Nant Derven.

Llanddewibrefi seemed to Borrow an apt place for retirement. It is certainly very quiet today, but in the past it has been the host of important events in ecclesiastical history. It was here that Dewi Sant or Saint David refuted the Pelagian heresy. Pelagius was a Welsh or possibly Irish monk of the late fourth and fifth centuries who denied the doctrine of original sin, maintaining, as Borrow puts it, 'that it is possible for a man to lead a life entirely free from sin by obeying the dictates of his own reason without any assistance from the grace of God.' It was only Dewi who could produce arguments powerful enough effectively to counter this doctrine. It is said that when he got up to address the assembly in the churchyard at Llanddewi the ground itself rose to bear him up above the crowd.

The church at Llanddewibrefi.

Llanddewi is famous too in legend. 'Here according to old tradition died one of the humped oxen of the team of Hu Gadarn.' Borrow says that the ox died 'distracted at having lost its comrade, which perished from the dreadful efforts [of] drawing the *afanc* from the lake of lakes', but there is a tradition which says that the oxen were engaged in dragging a huge stone to build the church at Llanddewi. One of them died in the effort and its bereaved partner gave a mighty bellow before it too died. *Brefu*, pronounced brevi as in Llanddewibrefi, means to bellow. Borrow tells us that 'horns of enormous size, said to have belonged to this humped ox or bison, were for many ages preserved in the church'. When he went to see the church, the old sexton told him that the horns had dwindled away to nothing, but he showed Borrow the memorial inscription of a very old man who had known another very old man who had once seen a tip of one of the horns. In fact the Welsh Folk Museum today preserves a horn-core known as *Mabcorn yr Ych Bannog* which comes from the church at Llanddewi. It is said to come from the species *Bos primogenius*, the ancient wild long-horned cattle of pre-Roman Britain.

Borrow travelled on to Lampeter, still on the B4343. He observed nothing remarkable on the way. At Lampeter he went to visit the college which was founded by Thomas Burgess in 1820 'for the education of youths intended for the ministry of the Church of England'. He mentions the library, now called the 'Founders Library' where he was shown a bloodstained volume:

> The grand curiosity is a manuscript Codex containing a Latin synopsis of Scripture which once belonged to the monks of Bangor Is Coed. It bears marks of blood with which it was sprinkled when the monks were massacred by the heathen Saxons, at the instigation of Austin, the Pope's missionary in Britain.

Gastineau's view of Lampeter College from *Wales Illustrated in a Series of Views*.

It is still possible for visitors to view the very book, *Distinctiones theologicae*, though it is by no means of the antiquity or the provenance that Borrow suggests. The text is by Peter of Capua who died in 1242. The volume certainly bears marks which are convincingly like bloodstains, but they have never scientifically been confirmed as such. The college at Lampeter is now part of the University of Wales. Borrow says that in his day the number of students seldom exceeded forty. He doesn't mention whether he saw any of them at study in the library. It would have been surprising if he had for the college's founder had discouraged students from going to the library too often – in case they read too much.

Walking swiftly on from Lampeter on the A482, Borrow came to a tiny village with only six or seven houses, three of which seemed to be pubs. This was probably at OS 614438 where Tafarn Jem now stands. The three publicans tell Borrow that they have no great reason to complain of their circumstances and that they all manage to get a living despite being in such close competition. Presumably this can only have been on account of the business brought to them by thirsty drovers, for we are on a main droving route here. Borrow declined invitations from the bibulous trio to drink with them – the cost of buying three drinks for every one they bought him seemed excessive – and travelled on towards Pumsaint.

At Pumsaint he stayed at the Dolaucothi Arms Hotel, 'a comfortable old-fashioned place' and 'a good specimen of an ancient Welsh hostelry'. Then as now it was part of the Dolaucothi estate which passed into the care of the National Trust in 1944. The building across the road from the hotel, now a visitor centre which houses a small exhibition, was built in 1833 and would have been a coach house in Borrow's time. The blacksmith's shop 'a little distance up the road' dates from at least 1756 and is still there now in use as a garage. He says nothing about the Roman occupation of this area and the nearby gold mines which they were the first to work. In fact the remains of the small Roman fort of *Loventinum* were discovered near to the hotel when the road was widened in the early 1970s.

Pumsaint today, showing the old forge on the right. The village derives its name from five saints, pilgrims who rested here on their way to St Davids.

The following morning Borrow visited the grounds of a nearby gentleman's seat, Dolaucothi House which was demolished in 1955. Delighted by the noble oaks and beautiful brook, the fine wooded hills and the plain but comfortable house, he exclaims:

> With what satisfaction I could live in that house . . . if backed by a couple of thousand a year. With what gravity could I sign a warrant in its library, and with what dreamy comfort translate an ode of Lewis Glyn Cothi, my tankard of rich ale beside me.

The house's real incumbent, John Johnes, a relation of the Johnes of Hafod, was described by the *Dictionary of Welsh Biography* as an 'able lawyer, keen agriculturalist and antiquary', but he turned out not to be so fortunate after all. In August 1876 he was murdered by his butler.

The name Dolaucothi, or Dol Cothi as he renders it, had put Borrow in mind of Lewis Glyn Cothi, 'the greatest poet after ab Gwilym of all Wales'. He lived from about 1420 to 1489, the troubled times of the Wars of the Roses. Borrow has already introduced us to him in Chapter 3 and quoted him on the slopes of Pumlumon in Chapter 88. More than two hundred of Lewis Glyn Cothi's poems have survived and of these 154 were published by the Cymmrodorion Society in 1837. Interestingly, one of the editors of this publication was Walter Davies, or Gwallter Mechain whom Borrow claims never before to have heard of in chapter 69 at Llanrhaeadr.

The Castle Hotel where Borrow stayed in Llandovery.

From Dolaucothi, Borrow continued down the A482 which follows the course of the Afon Dulais. At Llanwrda, which he describes as 'a pretty village with a singular-looking church', he turned left for Llandovery which he reached at about half past two. He crossed the Tywi by means of a 'noble suspension bridge' which survived until its replacement by the present bridge in 1883. At Llandovery he stayed at the Castle Inn where his visit is still recorded. The hotel retains the bed which they say is the very one he slept in.

Borrow describes the town as

> Small but beautiful ... situated amidst fertile meadows. It is a water-girdled spot, whence its name Llandovery or Llanymdyfri, which signifies the church surrounded by water. On its west is the Towey, and on its east the river Bran or Brein, which descending from certain lofty mountains to the north-east runs into the Towey a little way below the town. The most striking object which Llandovery can show is its castle ...

At this point he introduces Gruffudd ap Nicholas, 'one of the most remarkable men which South Wales has ever produced.' He was a man of divided loyalties: 'Though holding offices of trust and emolument under the Saxon, he in the depths of his soul detested the race and would have rejoiced to see it utterly extirpated from Britain.' The Penal Code imposed by the English following Glyndŵr's uprising forbade Welshmen from holding offices of any importance. It thus became necessary for the ambitious Welshman to petition parliament to make him an Englishman if he wished to procure advancement for himself. Gruffudd ap Nicholas had pursued this course which no doubt explains his contradictory position. He was legally English, but culturally Welsh. The 'congress of bards and literati at Carmarthen', to which Borrow alludes was the eisteddfod of 1451 where the Twenty-four Metres of Welsh prosody were agreed.

The most striking object which Llandovery can show: The imposing ruins of its castle.

While he was at Llandovery, Borrow attended a church service at Llanfair which is on the north-east edge of the town. It is here that William Williams Pantycelyn the great Methodist hymn writer is buried. It seems unlikely that Borrow was unaware of this, but he doesn't mention him at all. In a conversation with the church clerk he does however mention the Church of England incumbent at Llandovery, a man called Hughes, brother of the vicar at Tregaron and a worthy man against whom the dissenters themselves have nothing to say. Even he though is not to be compared to Rhys Prichard or 'yr Hen Ficer' (The Old Vicar).

It is thought that Rhys Prichard was born in 1579 at Old Neuadd which is now 33, High Street. He was appointed to the living of Llandovery in 1602. At first he was so inordinately addicted to drunkenness that 'his conduct for a considerable time was not only unbecoming a clergyman but a human being in any sphere . . . He was in the habit of spending the greater part of his time in the public-house, from which he was generally trundled home in a wheelbarrow in a state of utter insensibility'. He did offer his congregation a consolation of a sort, not through Christian ministration, it was more through the comparison they were able to make between themselves and the man of God: 'Bad as we may be we are not half so bad as the parson'. This debauchery could not go on. The people of the pub which he used to frequent kept a goat which mingled with the customers. One night Prichard called this animal to him and offered it drink from his tankard. The goat readily accepted and having become drunk fell senseless to the floor. His fellow drinkers were rather shocked, but Prichard, delighted, continued to drink until he too became insensible and had to be wheeled home in the customary manner.

> During the whole of the next day he was very ill and kept at home, but on the following one he again repaired to the public-house, sat down and called for his pipe and tankard. The goat was now perfectly recovered and was standing nigh. No sooner was the tankard brought than Rees taking hold of it held it to the goat's mouth. The creature, however, turned away its head in disgust and hurried out of the room. This circumstance produced an instantaneous effect upon Rees Pritchard:- 'My God!' said he to himself, 'is this poor dumb creature wiser than I? Yes, surely; it has been drunk, but having once experienced the wretched consequences of drunkenness, it refuses to be drunk again. How different is its conduct to mine!'

'Smashing his pipe', Borrow continues, 'he left his tankard untasted on the table, went home, and became an altered man'. Not only did he become a great preacher, he also composed Christian verses which were published as *Cannwyll y Cymry* (The Candle of the Welsh) in 1681 and which achieved enduring popularity.

Borrow went to see vicar Prichard's house, Neuadd Newydd or New Hall, which was on a site near the Blue Bell. He describes it as 'a very large mansion of dark red brick . . . It is in a very dilapidated condition and is inhabited at present by various poor families'. Part of the building was demolished in 1904, but part of it survived long enough to be photographed by Cecil Price for Collins' centennial edition of *Wild Wales,* albeit as a ruin. There is a monument to Rhys Prichard behind the altar in the church at Llandingad. The town's primary school is named after him and there is also a memorial hall.

Vicar Prichard's house from an engraving by W. Rees. Close observation shows a wheelbarrow parked outside, perhaps the very one in which the inebriate vicar was transported home from the pub!

CHAPTER TWELVE

Llandovery to Chepstow

Borrow departed from Llandovery on 10 November, paying it the tribute of having been 'the pleasantest little town' he had stayed in during the course of his wanderings. He took the route of the A4069 which runs south of the Tywi. When he reached Llangadog, a downpour of rain forced him to take refuge in an 'ancient-looking hostelry', perhaps the Black Lion – there are another three pubs in a row here in this thirsty village, which is also on the drovers' route. There he found the landlady to be 'a bitter Methodist, as bitter as her beer', though whether she added wormwood to her brew he does not say. He walked south from Llangadog heading for the Black Mountain. Somewhere in the region of Pontarllechau he admired the scenery:

I came to a glen, the sides of which were beautifully wooded.

> I came to a glen, the sides of which were beautifully wooded. On my left was a river, which came roaring down from a range of lofty mountains right before me to the south-east.

He came to 'a pretty village' on his right, 'something in the shape of a semicircle', which must have been the little settlement at OS 728 213, but there is no sign now of the fulling mill at the foot of the Black Mountain where

Afon Sawdde which rises on the Black Mountain.

he met 'a decent-looking man engaged in sawing a piece of wood by the roadside'. This man mistakes Borrow for a north Welshman and can hardly believe he has met so outlandish a species. We have already seen how Borrow was jeered at for being a bumpkin at Pontrhydygroes.

As he was about to ascend the Black Mountain, Borrow encountered the gypsies Captain and Mrs Bosvile. There has been much speculation as to why gypsy Borrow, the author of *Lavengro*, the *Romany Rye* and the *Zincali or the Gypsies in Spain,* should mention only one encounter with gypsies in *Wild Wales*. Wales was after all famous for its gypsies. It has been suggested that he did meet with many more gypsies than he reports, but omitted to write about them because his wife did not approve of them. Alternatively, it was a bourgeois reading public that he did not wish to offend. Cecil Price suggests that he included only one scene with gypsies 'to refute the critics of Lavengro, who had said that he was only at home in the gypsy life'. It seems that the truth may be even simpler than this, that Borrow really did only once encounter gypsies because there were very few of them in Wales in the mid-nineteenth century, they having been displaced by immigrants from Ireland. This is very much what John Jones reports in chapter 14 when he says that 'the Gwyddelod made their appearance in these parts about twenty years ago, and since then the Gipsiaid have been rarely seen'. Captain Bosvile himself says 'The country is overrun with Hindity mescrey, woild Irish, with whom the Romany foky stand no chance'.

Looking north from the Black Mountain.

In his conversation with the gypsies Borrow makes veiled, jocular references to his earlier work. When asked about Jasper Petulengro, Captain Bosvile replies: 'Lord! You can't think what grand folks he and his wife have become of late years, and all along of a trumpery lil which somebody has written about them.' The 'trumpery lil' is Borrow's *Lavengro*.

Borrow's description of his route is a little confusing to follow. He mentions Capel Gwynfe which is at OS 723 220 and which comes before the semicircular shaped village, not after it as he puts it. Similarly he writes of a huge chalk cliff towering over him on the right and a chalk precipice on his left as he is ascending the mountain. His description much better fits the road as you descend it on the other side of the mountain. Whatever slight failures there may have been in his memory or his notes, there is little doubt that he toiled up the not inconsiderable Black Mountain as night was approaching and a mist came swirling down. At one point a train of carts went rattling past him, the wheels dangerously close to his feet. Near to the top of the mountain there is a lone sad gravestone, which marks the death of a young farm worker. He was killed in the late nineteenth century when he was thrown from his horse and crushed beneath the wheels of his cart. No similar misfortune befell Borrow but he must have been very glad when, benighted and soaked to the skin, he reached the 'blaze of light' that heralded his 'much needed haven of rest', the tavern of Gutter Fawr, or Brynaman, in the county of Glamorgan.

The kitchen, or what we would now call the public bar, in the pub at Brynaman was full of miners and carters, a rough set according to one of the landlady's daughters. They were all 'whistling, singing, shouting or jabbering', but they fell silent the moment Borrow entered the room. 'Every eye was turned upon him with a strange inquiring stare'. It is a scene rather like the one in the pub at Cemais, but when Borrow introduces himself politely the men become quite friendly and welcoming. It is only later when they begin to suspect that Borrow understands rather more Welsh than he has let on that they turn a little hostile. He, however, proves more than equal to the occasion. First entertaining the company to an account of his experiences of Russia and Turkey, he goes on to recount Lope de Vega's ghost story, 'the grand ghost story of the world'. There is no space for the whole of that here, but it has been researched by Borrow's earliest biographer Dr Knapp and an extract from the beginning of the story is reproduced here in Borrow's own hand.

At Brynaman, Borrow had reached industrial South Wales and he went to see a nearby iron foundry before departing for Swansea. He passed through Llangiwg and Pontardawe noticing more iron works as he went. Somewhere south of Pontardawe he fell in step with Pat Flannagan, a pugnacious Irishman who pines for more violent days of old. Borrow is able to trade on the boyhood times he spent in Ireland and persuades his companion that he comes from Munster. There is an interesting variation in this episode on the theme of being mistaken for a priest, for Pat Flannagan mistakes Borrow for someone who couldn't quite manage the priesthood on account of his being 'over fond of the drop'.

At Swansea, Borrow put up at the Mackworth Arms in Wind Street. The accommodation was very good but the town itself he found large, bustling, dirty and gloomy. He continues:

> The town is of considerable size, with some remarkable edifices, spacious and convenient quays, and a commodious harbour into which the river Tawy flowing from the north empties itself.

He makes much of the Flemish origin of Swansea's people. Historically Tenby is the most Flemish of the towns on the south coast of Wales, but Flemings also settled on the Gower Peninsula. Wind Street, where Borrow stayed, is pronounced 'Wine' Street. At one time it housed the shops of the town's wine

Ancient and modern in Swansea today.

merchants. It was bombed during the Second World War, but a good deal of it survives and today it caters for the thirsty as much as ever. Even the banks have been converted into fashionable drinking premises.

From Swansea, Borrow headed north east to Neath. As he strode up the valley he was struck by the contrast between natural beauty and industrial artifice. 'There was a singular mixture of nature and art, of the voices of birds and the clanking of chains, of the mists of heaven and the smoke of furnaces'. He was horrified by the industrial scenery and uses images which equate it with hell. Nothing could prepare him for the scene which presented itself as he drew near to Neath Abbey:

> Somewhat to the south rose immense stacks of chimneys surrounded by grimy diabolical-looking buildings, in the neighbourhood of which were huge heaps of cinders and black rubbish. From the chimneys, not withstanding it was Sunday, smoke was proceeding in volumes, choking the atmosphere all around. From this pandemonium, at the distance of about a quarter of a mile to the south-west, upon a green meadow, stood, looking darkly grey, a ruin of vast size with window holes, towers, spires and arches.

Neath Abbey. The ruins are still surrounded by an industrial estate.

Between it and the accursed pandemonium, lay a horrid filthy place, part of which was swamp and part pool: the pool black as soot, and the swamp of a disgusting leaden colour. Across this place of filth stretched a tramway leading seemingly from the abominable mansions to the ruin. So strange a scene I had never beheld in nature. Had it been on canvas, with the addition of a number of diabolical figures, proceeding along the tramway, it might have stood for Sabbath in Hell – devils proceeding to afternoon worship, and would have formed a picture worthy of the powerful but insane painter Jerome Bos [Hieronymus Bosch].

From Neath, Borrow continued in a north-easterly direction up the vale. He describes the scenery as very beautiful, marred only by 'one of those detestable contrivances a railroad'. He went through Rhigos which is now to the south of today's main road , the A465, and mentions Irvan which is probably Hirwaun, now the site of Tower Colliery, the only surviving deep coal mine in Wales. There he noted 'a spectral-looking chapel, doubtless a Methodist one' and 'rough savage-looking men'. As he approached Merthyr Tydfil he saw a hill glowing with the dross from the iron forges. He entered the town amidst blazes from the ironworks and gives us a brief glimpse of the terrible living conditions which were prevalent at the time.

I went through a filthy slough, over a bridge, and up a street, from which dirty lanes branched off on either side, passed throngs of savage-looking people talking clamourously.

General view over Mythyr Tydfil.

The industrial work force arrived in Merthyr long before modern sanitation and drainage. Dwellings were squalid and unhealthy. In 1854, the year of Borrow's tour, there were 455 deaths from cholera, four times as many as in Cardiff and nine times as many as in Neath.

Despite his horror of industrialism, Borrow nevertheless visited and reported on the sights of the place like the great Cyfarthfa Ironworks, but he does so without eagerness:

What shall I say about the Cyfarthfa Fawr? I had best say but very little.

He doesn't have the same enthusiasm for communicating all the details to the reader as he does with the bards and the historical characters of the north. In Merthyr he notes 'a truly wonderful edifice';

A house of reddish brick with a slate roof – four horrid black towers behind, two of them belching forth smoke and flame from their tops – holes like pigeon holes here and there – two immense white chimneys standing by themselves. What edifice can that be of such strange but mad details? I ought to have put that question to someone in Tydvil, but did not . . .

He shrank from the people as well as the architecture in the south, but if he is reticent with the populations of the industrial towns, he gives us full measure of extraordinary characters on the open road. Pat Flannagan we have already met. The whole of Chapter 105 is given over to the story of Johanna Colgan, the 'bedivilled woman from the county of Limerick'. On the road from Newport to Chepstow he encounters the Irish girl he had first met on the green near Chester with the tinker Tourlough and his wife. Perhaps he places her here at the end of his journey to link the beginning of the book with the end and so wrap the whole thing up.

Cyfarthfa Castle, built by the Crawshay family, owners of the Cyfarthfa Ironworks, in 1824.

George Childs' watercolour of 1840 shows the Dowlais Ironworks.

129

Caerphilly Castle on a winter's evening.

From Merthyr Borrow travelled to Caerphilly via Troed y Rhiw and Ystrad Mynach. He stayed at the Boar's Head, conveniently close to the castle. Caerphilly Castle, as Borrow says, is a truly enormous structure. The whole site covers thirty acres. The Romans were the first to establish a fort here, but it was Gilbert de Clare, not John de Bryse as Borrow tells us, who began the construction of the present castle in 1268. De Clare was a powerful Marcher baron who sought to resist the increasing influence of Llywelyn ap Gruffudd. The castle was built on the concentric pattern later to be used at Edwardian castles like Beaumaris with successive lines of defence, both aquatic and mural, set one inside the other. Later on, in the early fourteenth century it belonged to the Spencers, more correctly the Despencers, who sheltered the unfortunate Edward II in 1326. The Great Hall, 'the grand banqueting room' which Borrow mentions has recently been restored. It is not certain as he reports that Cromwell ruined the castle though it is thought that it saw some action in the Civil War. The well-known 'leaning tower' may well be the result of an explosion at that time, but could equally have been caused by subsidence.

The characteristic leaning tower.

From Caerphilly, Borrow headed east for Newport, crossing the river Rhymney and taking the route now followed by the A 468. He passed through Machen and Bassaleg (Basallaig) to reach Newport in the late afternoon where he put up at the 'large and handsome King's Head'. The Sir Charles to whom he refers along the way was Sir Charles Morgan of Tredegar, the substantial landowner of these parts who had branched out from agriculture into iron working, transport and shipping. His son, whom a road mender tells Borrow 'is in the Crimea fighting the Roosiaid' actually took part in the Charge of the Light Brigade. His former seat, Tredegar House Country Park, is on the south-west edge of Newport beneath the constant thunder of the M4.

Roman foundations at Caer-went.

Borrow took the route of the A48 (T) to Chepstow. He mentions Pen-how where he saw Pen-how Castle which sits on the lower of two knolls and a 'sharp pointed blue mountain away to the north-west. Llanfaches he notes as 'a pretty little village' but Caer-went appeared to him 'a poor desolate place consisting of a few old-fashioned houses and a strange-looking dilapidated church'. It was once, as he says, an important Roman station, *Venta Silurum.* An inscripted stone in the church porch at Caer-went dates from the early third century. The Roman basilica was just to the north of the road which runs through the middle of today's village, the public baths just to the south.

At Chepstow, Borrow had reached the end of his journey. He went to the principal hotel and ordered the best dinner available and then visited the castle and drank water from the mouth of the river Wye, just as he had drunk from its source a few weeks before. After dinner he whiled the time away over a bottle of port before catching the ten o'clock train to London.

In his notebook he wrote 'End of my wanderings in Wales: Chepstow, Thursday, night, November 16, 1854 – George Borrow'. On 17 November 1854 he wrote to his wife from 53A Pall Mall:

> I arrived here at about 5 o'clock this morning. Since I saw you I have walked about 250 miles . . .

The Wye at Chepstow makes stately progress to the sea. The elegant bridge which links Wales to England was already decades old by Borrow's time.

Notes on Sources and Further Reading

Apart from *Wild Wales*, Borrow's major works are *The Bible in Spain*, *The Gypsies of Spain*, *Lavengro* and *The Romany Rye*. He also published a translation of Ellis Wynne's *Visions of the Sleeping Bard* in 1862 and he wrote a companion volume to *Wild Wales*, entitled *Celtic Bards, Chiefs and Kings* which was not published until 1929. The notebooks on which *Wild Wales* is based are in the library of the Hispanic Society of America in New York, except for eighteen pages in the Ashley Collection in the British Library's Department of Manuscripts. However, substantial published extracts can be found in Angus M. Fraser 'George Borrow's Wild Wales: Fact and Fabrication', *Transactions of the Honourable Society of Cymmrodorion*, 1980 and 'George Borrow's Walking Tours: The Welsh Diary 2-6 Sept 1854', *Journal of the Gypsy Lore Society*, Third Series XLIX, 1970, by the same author.

There have been many biographies of George Borrow, but it is probably fair to say that his first biographer has not yet been surpassed. William I. Knapp's *Life, Writings and Correspondence of George Borrow* appeared in 1899, published by John Murray. I have also found Herbert Jenkins's, *The Life of George Borrow*, John Murray (1912) both interesting and useful; similarly, *George Borrow as a Lingyuist* (Warborough). An essential resource for the student of Borrow is the *George Borrow Bulletin*, published twice yearly by the George Borrow Society. Subscription details can be obtained by writing to the Membership Secretary, Mr Michael Skillman, 60 Upper Marsh Road, Warminster, Wiltshire BA12 9PN.

From the wealth of general, historical and topographical literature on Wales, I would select the following three: Jan Morris *Wales*, Penguin Books (1980), John Davies *A History of Wales*, Penguin Books (1994) and William Condry *Exploring Wales*, Faber and Faber (1972). The local studies I have found particularly useful include Gordon Sherratt *An Illustrated History of Llangollen* Ceiriog Press (2000), Jim Roberts, *Snowdonia* Sutton Publishing (2000), David Wyn Davies *A Pictorial History of Machynlleth*, Machynlleth and district Civil Society (1996), Darrell Kingerlee *Llandovery Album*, Llandovery Publications (1985).

On Borrow and Welsh literature, I would not have been without Ann M. Ridler *George Borrow as a Linguist: Images and Contexts* (1996). Also indispensable has been *The New Companion to the Literature of Wales*, compiled and edited by Meic Stephens, University of Wales Press 1998. The same author's The Literary Pilgrim in Wales, Gwasg Carreg Gwalch (2000), is interesting too and much more pocketable. Those who seek detailed studies of Welsh poets will find *Iolo Goch* and *Dafydd ap Gwilym* in Gwasg Gomer's The Welsh Classics series complete with introductions, notes and English translations.

Cadw, Welsh Historic Monuments, publish useful and beautifully illustrated guides to many of the castles and abbeys that Borrow visited, including Valle Crucis, Beaumaris, Strata Florida, Caerphilly and Caer Went. Chirk Castle is now in the care of the National Trust who publish their own informative guide book.

Picture Credits

Chester History and Heritage: 1
National Library of Wales: 4, 17, 34B., 35, 36, 71, 78, 79, 101, 108, 109T., 109B., 121
National Museums and Galleries of Wales: 29, 129
Jim Roberts: 41T.
Gordon Sherratt: 11T.,11B.
Jane Whittle: 58, 58-9
David Wyn Davies: 94
Wrexham Heritage Services: 7B.